HOMILIES ON THE HEART OF JESUS AND THE APOSTLESHIP OF PRAYER

BOOKS BY HERBERT F. SMITH, SJ

Living for Resurrection
God Day by Day
The Lord Experience
The Pilgrim Contemplative
How to Get What You Want from God
Hidden Victory (A Historical Novel of Jesus)
Prayer and Personality Development
Homosexuality (co-authored)
Sunday Homilies, Cycle A
Sunday Homilies, Cycle B
Sunday Homilies, Cycle C
Pro Choice? Pro Life? The questions, The answers
Natural Family Planning: Why It Succeeds

Visit our web site at
WWW.ALBAHOUSE.ORG

"The Holy Father has called for a New Evangelization that started where it all began: the Heart of Christ. Fr. Smith calls Christians back to the love that animates the world and writes with a wisdom that was developed and formed by many years of prayer. May many hearts respond to the message."

Thomas M. King, SJ, Professor of Theology, Georgetown University, Co-Founder of the National University Professors for Life and recently nominated by the staff of *The Hoya* "Georgetown's Man of the Century."

"If Catholicism is to flourish in our culture, there must be a profound, incisive and well-formulated theological teaching balanced by a healthy, moderated, nourishing and affective devotional life. Theology minus affectivity can be dry, sterile and boring, whereas a devotional life unbalanced leads often to sentimentalism, superstition and cultism. Fr. Smith attempts to balance this difficult task in his *Homilies on the Heart of Jesus and the Apostleship of Prayer: The Apostleship of Prayer for the World's Salvation*. This book presents a challenge to every priest, Sister, Brother and lay person to look at today's Church longing for a balanced theological-devotional life. Some lay people are finding this nourishment in sects, others are asking for it in their parishes."

John Rainaldo, SJ, National Director of the Apostleship of Prayer-Sacred Heart Devotion

Homilies on the
Heart of Jesus and the
Apostleship of Prayer

The Apostleship of Prayer for the World's Salvation

HERBERT F. SMITH, SJ

ALBA·HOUSE house NEW·YORK

SOCIETY OF ST. PAUL, 2187 VICTORY BLVD., STATEN ISLAND, NEW YORK 10314

ST PAULS

Library of Congress Cataloging-in-Publication Data

Smith, Herbert F.
    Homilies on the Heart of Jesus and the Apostleship of Prayer : the Apostleship of
Prayer for the world's salvation / Herbert F. Smith.
        p. cm.
    Includes bibliographical references.
    ISBN 0-8189-0844-0
    1. Sacred Heart, Devotion to—Sermons. 2. Apostleship of Prayer (Organization) 3.
Catholic Church—Sermons. 4. Sermons, American. I. Title.

    BX2157.S65 2000
    252'.02—dc21

                                                        00-021328

Imprimi Potest:
James R. Stormes, SJ
Provincial Superior, Society of Jesus
Maryland Province
Baltimore, April 26, 1999

Nihil Obstat:
Msgr. Francis A. Barszczewski
Censor Librorum
May 14, 1999

Imprimatur:
✠ Anthony Cardinal Bevilacqua
Archbishop of Philadelphia
May 17, 1999

The Nihil Obstat and Imprimatur are a declaration that a book or pamphlet is considered
to be free from doctrinal or moral error. It is not implied that those who have granted the
Nihil Obstat and Imprimatur agree with the contents, opinions or statements expressed.

Produced and designed in the United States of America by the
Fathers and Brothers of the Society of St. Paul,
2187 Victory Boulevard, Staten Island, New York 10314-6603,
as part of their communications apostolate.

ISBN: 0-8189-0844-0

Printing Information:

Current Printing - first digit   1   2   3   4   5   6   7   8   9   10

Year of Current Printing - first year shown

2000   2001   2002   2003   2004   2005   2006   2007   2008   2009

DEDICATED

To the Board of Directors of the Apostleship of Prayer
who have committed to wide distribution
of this volume in token of the author's contributions
to spreading the eternal devotion to the Heart of Jesus
into the Third Christian Millennium.

THE MASTER

Come to me, all you who labor and are burdened, and I will give you rest. Take my yoke upon you and learn from me, for I am meek and humble of heart; and you will find rest for yourselves. For my yoke is easy and my burden light (Mt 11:28-30, *Lectionary For Sunday Masses*, 1998).

THE DISCIPLE

Our Savior from the Father's side, Lord of all the world, save us by your side and Heart once pierced, save us by your death and rising. Call us, Shepherd Jesus, to follow you and find salvation. Lead us to the pasture of life's food, and gather us into one flock in your own sheepfold. Guard us from the foe, and guide us to our Father's house.

CONTENTS

FOREWORD

This foreword provides the author's insights into how the homilies that follow can be used more effectively. It also attunes the reader to use well a unique feature, the *Homiletic Realizations* which preface each homily.

A homilist-author must have good reason to think his homilies can be of service to others. It may be that he has had the opportunity of devoting more time to the preparation of each homily than the average priest can dream of doing. It may be that he has specialized in the field in which the homilies are concentrated, spending hours and years in the study and research that alone can bring due competence. Both reasons prevail here.

The idea for the *Homiletic Realizations* derives from many sources: the priestly prayer of Aquinas found in the Preparation for Mass in the Roman altar missal; the practice of the Fathers of the Church as evidenced in their homilies; the instinctual realization of any gifted preacher concerning his role as preacher and the reasons for choosing what he is including in his homily and what he is omitting. A look at these reasons will facilitate able use of the *Realizations*.

In St. Thomas's prayer of preparation for Mass, he begs God for the grace to be healed, saying "I come sick to the doctor of life, unclean to the fountain of mercy." Can we doubt that the priestly people who are at the Masses at which we preach need the same grace, and that our homilies must help them find it?

The Fathers of the Church are courageous in saying what needs to be said when they preach; and sometime the *Homiletic Realizations* which compel them to speak with such boldness propel their way into the homily itself. The Office for the 24th week of the year presents a prime example of this in the second reading, drawn from St. Augustine's sermon *On Pastors*. In it he speaks of the scriptural warning to "shepherds who feed themselves and not the sheep," and how this guides his own way of preaching.

Our homily on the scriptural readings of the day is often drawn from the remedy which the divine Physician presents in the Gospel passage. But "Every scribe who has been instructed in the kingdom of God is like the head of a household who brings from his storeroom both the new and the old" (Mt 13:52). That is, we have to add to the Lord's remedy whatever potion is required by the contemporary variations of the specific illness being treated. That is why this author prefaces each homily with the *Homiletic Realizations* that will help homilists who use it to better share the involvement of the mind and the impulses of the heart which created it and are needed to deliver it effectively.

Good homilies are not prepared or given without talent and hard work, but that is not enough. We need the help of the Holy Spirit. It is the author's intention and hope that the homilists who read this book will be inspired by the *Homiletic Realizations* to take the contents to prayer and meditation and the Holy Spirit to plead for the needed help. For it was prayer and meditation which originated the mental involvement and movements of the heart which produced the homilies, and from prayer and meditation they can arise afresh to enable their living re-creation.

One particular *Realization* influences the bulk of these homilies. It is that we priests and Deacons must appreciate anew the value of popular devotions in the Church, practice and promote them, and recognize that their precipitous decline in the last several decades is a grave loss. For who will certify that this decline is not a factor significantly contributing to the precipitous decline in attendance at Mass during the same decades?

Both declines followed the Second Vatican Council, but both contradict the Council. In *The Constitution on the Sacred Liturgy* the Council calls the sacred liturgy the summit of all the Church's activity; then it adds that it is not the whole of the spiritual life. It calls for private prayer, and declares that "Popular devotions of the Christian people are warmly commended, provided that they accord with the laws and norms of the Church. Such is especially the case with devotions called for by the Apostolic See" (#13). Further, seminarians being formed in the spiritual life "need to celebrate the sacred mysteries personally, as well as popular devotions which are animated with the spirit of the liturgy" (#17).

Devotion to the Heart of Jesus, and membership in the Apostleship of Prayer (which is its most powerful advocate) are pre-eminently called for by the Apostolic See. This will become manifest in the Introduction that follows.

Fr. Peter-Hans Kolvenbach, S.J., the Director General of the Apostleship of Prayer, in a September, 1989, address to its leaders, treated this topic of heartfelt devotion in the Church. "It appears to me," he said, "that the Church's liturgy stresses more and more that one cannot be Christian without the spirituality of the heart." He declared that "the intentions of the Apostleship of Prayer should be expressions of the passion of God for mankind." He refers to the "mystery" of the decline of devotions following Vatican II "with none to replace them." He adds "And now, as Cardinal Ratzinger has affirmed in a recent article, if the Church herself refrains from showing 'pathos,' it is no surprise to find so many pathological signs."

It is well-known that many Catholics have wandered from the Church to Christian sects which propagate forms of worship that stir their feelings and their hearts, as Catholic practices like the Holy Hour did for so many for so long.

That the decline of popular devotions have other serious consequences in need of remedy becomes clear if we ponder the distinction and the interconnection between *devotions* and *devotion*. *Devotions* are the formal and informal practices of prayer and services that help us approach the Lord and his Saints. *Devotion* is **the readiness to do God's will in all things.** It is the flowering of true love. Since solid Devotions move the heart to devotion, it is evident why the decline of devotions is disastrous.

When it comes to devotion to the Heart of Jesus, Devotions and devotion virtually merge. An example will illustrate this. A fellow priest, speaking about his experience guiding the faithful, said that in today's confused world the faithful are confused even about the sense and meaning of their lives.

I responded, "That is why I value the Apostleship of Prayer so highly. In the Daily Offering, we give all we do and experience to the Lord. He knows what to do with it."

That is what Fr. Walter Ciszek found was true even in Lubianka (See his account in the Introduction). That is what Devotions can lead us to do: accept everything, even without understanding it, and give it to the Lord. That is what devotion to the Heart of Jesus does, especially when it is practiced according to the Ignatian spirituality of the Apostleship of Prayer.

And what the *Homiletic Realizations* in this book can do is help the user of the homilies see and feel the why and wherefore of each homily of which they are emissaries.

INTRODUCTION

Why the Heart of Jesus and the Apostleship of Prayer? Why a new book of homilies on the Heart of Jesus and the Apostleship of Prayer, the League of the Heart of Jesus?

And why that pretentious-sounding subtitle, *The Apostleship of Prayer for the World's Salvation?* Could not a more informative subtitle have been used, like "Homilies for Sundays, Feasts, Novenas, and Retreats"? The answer is that the subtitle conveys in eight words profound information about the Apostleship of Prayer that is not in the least exaggerated: that is its purpose and mission from the beginning. It represents the purpose of the founder, who had a vision that has been validated, and will gradually appear in these pages. It also appears in the post-Vatican II Statutes of the Apostleship of Prayer, which tell us that the Apostleship of Prayer is a way for the faithful, by their daily oblation, to "unite themselves with the Eucharistic Sacrifice" and so "cooperate in the redemption of the world" (I).

Are devotion to the Heart of Jesus and its attendant spirituality as practiced in the Apostleship of Prayer important for the 21st century of the Christian era? The facts require a resounding affirmative. How can we present those facts here briefly but convincingly? *What is the evidence?* Is it enough to state the simple fact that the Pierced Side is a focal point of the Bible, that Jesus himself calls us to the devotion, that Popes for a century urge both the devotion and the Apostleship of Prayer, that Saints can be named who resoundingly praise and commend them and mystics who were on fire with them, that theological scholars and geniuses urge them, that tens of millions of Catholics practice them, and that the good they have generated in the past is an unassailable advocate for their future use?

In the light of these facts, one might consider it a waste of time even to respond to the contention that devotion to the Heart of Jesus is a relic of the past. The evidence justifies the assertion that the devotion is important for the 21st century and for eternity! But the task of supporting that assertion by further evidence is imposed by preachers and teachers who have implicitly denied the importance of the devotion to the Heart of Jesus by neglecting both the devotion and the Apostleship of Prayer.

The mystery is that the importance of devotion to the Heart of the Savior could be questioned. Among the last things are death and judgment, heaven and hell. Death and judgment will pass, but devotion to the Heart of Jesus will never pass. It will coexist with heaven, for all found worthy of heaven will practice it there. As St. Augustine says, "Things are said to be at home when they are in place, and the place of the human heart is the Heart of God."

That is the panoramic answer to our question, Why the Heart of Jesus and the Apostleship of Prayer? It is time now to look at some particular evidence in favor of the devotion and the Apostleship given us by Jesus and by his vicars, by Saints and theologians, by scholars and by the people.

Jesus first. Jesus himself has called us to devotion to his Heart, both in public and private revelation. Altogether familiar are his words from Matthew's Gospel so frequently used in the Church's worship: "Come to me, all you who labor and are burdened, and I will give you rest. Take my yoke upon you and learn from me, for I am meek and humble of heart; and you will find rest for yourselves. For my yoke is easy and my burden light" (Mt 11:28-30, N.A.B., the translation used in the new 1998 *Lectionary For Sunday*). Where else can one find a call so personal, tender, and full of feeling? He who is the "Everlasting Father" Isaiah foretold is opening his arms and inviting his hard-pressed children to a heart-felt embrace.

His call has a depth never to be plumbed. It summons each disciple to go beyond verbal descriptions of the way of salvation to seeing and following him as The Living Way and The Living Truth, for he is The Life. It is the call to participate in the love-life of God himself as it has come into the world incarnate in the Son.

In John's Gospel, Jesus couches the call to his Heart more mysteriously and mystically: "'Let anyone who thirsts come to me and drink. Whoever believes in me, as scripture says: "Rivers of living water will flow from within him."' He said this in reference to the Spirit that those who came to believe in him were to receive. There was, of course, no Spirit yet, because Jesus had not yet been glorified" (7:37-39). This prophetic utterance had antecedent prophecies in the Old Testament, as in Ezekiel 47:1. It referred of course to Jesus' glorification in his sacrificial death and resurrection. It had its fulfillment on Calvary: "One soldier thrust his lance into his side, and immediately blood and water flowed out" (Jn 19:34). Behold how Jesus has issued his invitation no longer in words, but in the unutterable manner of letting his breast be pierced and his Heart laid open to each who would come and be reborn in the water of the Spirit flowing forth, and nourished in the blood of the Eucharist, to be fit to enter into the home of love from which this new life has just poured out in the redemptive act.

Jesus also calls us to his Heart through his mystics. Names like St. Anselm of Canterbury, St. Bernard of Clairvaux, and St. Gertrude ring out. But it was St. Margaret Mary Alacoque to whom Jesus gave the most daunting task. She was to spread the devotion throughout the Church by promoting a worldwide feast of his Sacred Heart. The Feast and the well-known First Friday devotions were given her as a way to return love to his pierced and spurned Heart, and to make reparation for the sins against his love. Jesus sent her his "faithful servant and perfect friend," the Jesuit Father, St. Claude de la Colombiere, to guide and assist her in her mission.

St. Margaret Mary had a further vision after St. Claude died which has had a vast influence on the Church's Heart of Jesus devotion. Our Lady appeared to her, pointed to the Sisters of the Visitation on one side of her, and made them the guardians of the Sacred Heart devotion; then, to St. Claude on her other side, Our Lady declared that the Fathers of the Society of Jesus were given the noble task of showing and making known the usefulness and value of the treasured devotion to the Heart of her Son (July, 1688, recorded in

Letter 89 of St. Margaret Mary). This commission eventually led to the founding of the Apostleship of Prayer, the League of the Heart of Jesus.

The Apostleship of Prayer was born in a Jesuit house of studies in France. By deliberate choice and purpose it was born on December 3, 1844, the Feast of the great Jesuit missionary, St. Francis Xavier. The humble act of generating the Apostleship was the work of Jesuit Father Francis X. Gautrelet. He was spiritual director of Jesuit seminarians more eager to follow the inspiring footsteps of the great missionary than to fulfill their daily duty of studying to complete their priestly preparation. "Be apostles now, apostles of prayer!" Gautrelet urged. "Offer everything you are doing every day in union with the Heart of our Lord for what He wishes, the spread of his Kingdom for the salvation of souls. This is needed to win the graces essential for the propagation of the Faith." His vision took hold among the young men, and the Apostleship of Prayer was born.

Some years later the founder handed on the organization to the care of one who had been his student at its inception, Fr. Henry Ramiere. Ramiere's work has been called "epic-making," and has won him the title of "second founder." In 1859 he published his book, *The Apostleship of Prayer.* He gave it the subtitle, *A League of Christian Hearts united with the Sacred Heart of Jesus to obtain the salvation of the world and the triumph of the Church.*

It is one of the most powerful books on the prayer of petition every written. In it, Ramiere asks the disturbing question: Why are the elect so few? Why is the Incarnation seemingly so barren? He finds the root of his answer in St. Paul: "I ask that supplications, prayers, petitions and thanksgiving be offered for everyone" for God our Savior "wills everyone to be saved and to come to knowledge of the truth" (1 Tm 2:1-6). Ramiere's conclusion: If holiness of life, and prayer for everyone, is neglected by many in the Church, have we not found at least a partial answer to our troubling question?

But then, drawing on Paul again, he goes further: God wills to rely on the zeal and endeavors of all Christians to work with him: God does everything, but nothing alone, as a study of creation shows us.

He works through us as secondary causes, just as the Son of God worked through his *created human nature.*

Ramiere speaks of the power of association: When millions band together to do a task, how tremendously powerful! And when this power comes from union with the Heart of Jesus, the power becomes divine. He argues that *if Christians were doing what they ought, the association of the Apostleship of Prayer would be unnecessary.* But in fact it is needed to awaken them to the great truths and duties they neglect.

Ramiere goes on to describe how the Apostleship of Prayer will transform families and society itself: It will spread the spirit of love that will bring peace and well-being to states; keep alive the search for truth that leads to scientific development; lead to honest and devoted workers who will augment industrial productivity.

Though he didn't express it with the clarity that could come only a century later, Ramiere presents a vision of the Church of the future, the Church of our time. Today's Church is comprised of members who are gifted with better education, more democratic opportunities and wider influence than ever before in history. These members are coming to realize that the true nature of the Apostleship of Prayer is not just prayer but *prayer and service.* In our prayer we offer everything we do every day, and through our prayer we learn exactly what God wants us to do, and do better. And we do it, so that our lives, families, careers take new directions and take on the labors needed for the transformation and conversion of the world.

This brings us to the attitude of the vicars of Christ toward the Apostleship of Prayer and devotion to the Heart of Jesus. First, a brief summary of the papal view of the Apostleship as seen through the eyes of Pope John Paul II, then some details from other Popes.

John Paul II has pointed out that since the Apostleship's earliest years Popes have backed it. In 1994, in a letter that commemorated its 150th anniversary, he said to the Director General of the association that "The Apostleship of Prayer has always been especially close to the Roman Pontiffs. Pius IX approved its first statutes [in 1866] and exhorted its members to make the daily offering of their work and prayers for the intentions of the Church and the Pope. Every Pope since then has given special attention to this association, emphasizing the efficacious contribution it makes to apostolic activity.... The new evangelization will also be effective insofar as it strengthens the bonds of ecclesial communion with the grace that flows from the Heart of Christ."

Now, a look at individual Popes from Leo XIII on, to see some of the reasons for their unflagging support to the present.

In nine different briefs, Pope Leo XIII conferred various privileges on the Apostleship of Prayer. He was profoundly aware of the power of the devotion to the Heart of Jesus for the individual and the world.

The Church has endlessly praised *Rerum Novarum*, Leo's encyclical on capital and labor, and celebrated its centenary in 1981. But Leo XIII himself gave far more weight to his Sacred Heart encyclical, *Annum Sacrum*, released May 25, 1899. In a meeting with the bishop of Liège before he issued *Annum Sacrum*, he revealed his plan: "I am going to carry out the greatest act of my pontificate." He explained that he was going to ordain the consecration of the whole human race to the Heart of Jesus their King.[1] In the encyclical he writes of "the extraordinary and lasting benefits" for Christendom and the whole human race which he expected from the consecration.

Leo XIII saw with profound depth what Ramiere had been formulating when he advised joining everything to the Heart of Jesus. Leo envisioned help from that Heart to produce a development in society that would beggar the plans of the communists and bring peace and prosperity worldwide by a new involvement of the laity in God's plan for humanity. Leo's vision and his encyclical on labor, together with his *Annum Sacrum* consecrating the world to the Sacred Heart of Jesus, has been followed by a century of Popes further developing the social doctrine in the Church, and developing with it a new vision of lay activity that forms part of the concept of the *new evangelization* which Pope John Paul II has so stressed.

---

[1] "Sister Mary of the Divine Heart," 30 pp. (Augustine Publishing Company, Chulmleigh, Devon, 1988), pp. 24-25.

All of this is at home in the Apostleship of Prayer as it is in the Heart of Jesus. Just as a small sapling which grows into a great oak has only pursued the development of its own vital force, the Apostleship of Prayer stresses not only prayer, but prayer and service to bring into play the potential of its modern members. All who share the passion of the Heart of Christ for the well-being of his people in time and in eternity will not only pray but labor with their King and Lord to bring it about.

Pope St. Pius X said of the Apostleship of Prayer, "Catholics have established many very useful works, but none is more useful...."

Pope Benedict XV said that "no one should omit joining it." Pope Pius XI said that "all without exception should belong to it." Pope Pius XII wrote that "We call the League a perfect devotion to the Sacred Heart, so perfect that the two cannot be separated.... We, like our Predecessor of happy memory, Pius XI, have made known and once more most willingly declare that it will make Us very happy if all the Faithful without exception enlist in this sacred militia to swell the army of Associates now numbering 35,000,000."

Through his Secretary of State, Pope Paul VI conveyed his estimate of the Apostleship of Prayer: "without doubt [it] is to be numbered among the most salutary institutions which have arisen in the Church." He "commends this devoted association to all the children of the Church in whatsoever state of life they may be in." The Pope observes that Vatican II "has brought to light the brilliant mystery of the Holy Church. But this mystery can never be properly understood if the attention of the people is not drawn to that eternal love of the Incarnate Word, of which the wounded Heart of Jesus is the outstanding symbol." Quoting from Vatican II's teaching in the *Constitution on the Church* that the blood and water from the crucified Jesus' open side symbolize the Church's inauguration and growth (#3), the Pope declared that "The Church was born from the pierced Heart of the Redeemer and is nourished there.... Thus it is absolutely necessary that the faithful venerate and honor this Heart..." (Letter to various religious orders, May 25, 1968).

Pope John Paul II, who never tires of writing of the Heart of the Redeemer, addressed an April 13, 1985 meeting of the Apostleship of Prayer leaders. He praised the association for distinguishing itself "by its commitment to spread the devotion and the spirituality to the Heart of the Redeemer." He referred to the Sacred Heart encyclicals of Leo XIII and Pius XI, and then quoted from Pius XII's encyclical, *Haurietis Aquas*: "The Heart of Jesus is the Heart of a Divine Person, that is, of the Word Incarnate, and continues to put before our eyes all the love that he had and continues to have for us. For this reason, the cult of the Most Sacred Heart of Jesus must be held in such high esteem as to be considered as the most complete expression of the Christian religion."

John Paul II said in conclusion, "With these wishes I put this universal Pious Association into your hands as a precious treasure from the Pope's heart and the Heart of Christ. Put all your talents and all your strength in the accomplishment of this mission that I entrust to you today" (*L'Osservatore Romano*, April 29, 1985, p. 5).

In 1994, in a letter congratulating the General of the Society of Jesus on the 150th anniversary of the Apostleship of Prayer, the Pope affirmed the continuing importance of the Apostleship and the Heart of Jesus devotion when he wrote that "The new evangelization will also be effective insofar as it strengthens the bonds of ecclesial communion with the grace that flows from the Heart of Christ. The Apostleship of Prayer during the past century and a half has created a profound communion of prayer among hundreds of millions of believers. Nothing less is expected of it in the future." Like his predecessors for almost a century, the Pope in the same letter affirmed "the fundamental importance of this Apostolate within the Church universal as well as in the life of each and every one of the faithful."[2]

Since we are here answering the question, *Why the Heart of Jesus and the Apostleship of Prayer?*, it is appropriate in this context of the Popes' support to answer our question with a question: Can anyone name any other organization which Popes for a century and

---

[2] A fuller treatment of many of these papal quotes, plus their sources, can be found in Appendix Two.

to this day urge everyone to join, since it is of "fundamental importance... in the life of each and every one of the faithful"?

Theologians liberal, conservative and centered continue to affirm the great value of devotion to the Heart of Jesus. Among them is Cardinal Joseph Ratzinger. His book, *Behold The Pierced One: An Approach to a Spiritual Christology*, roots the devotion in the biblical-magisterial vision of the incarnate Son of God. Drawing on the scholarship of Fr. Hugo Rahner, he stresses the New Testament texts which center the devotion in the pierced side and the outflow of blood and water as the outpouring of the Spirit who conveys the resurrection life to the members of Christ's body. Hugo Rahner drew this interpretation directly from the Church Fathers' perception of the meaning of Christ pierced on the cross: "...from the Lord's pierced Heart proceeds the life-giving streams of the sacraments" (p. 48).

Fr. Teilhard de Chardin, S.J., was deeply attached to the Heart of Jesus devotion, which was a focal point for his vision of the created universe as a dynamic system of matter in motion working its way back to the Omega Point, God Himself. In the booklet, "Symbols, Devotions and Jesuits," his perceptions are summarized: In our religion of the Incarnation, the Incarnate Son becomes the Center and unifying force toward which everything is drawn as the cosmos moves toward the Parousia. Since we human beings have to work our way to God through matter, the flesh-and-blood matter of the Heart of Jesus is an immensely appealing and powerful way of drawing us to our Omega Point. Teilhard tried to use his insights to invigorate and promote devotion to the Heart of Jesus (pp. 31-39).

Fr. Edouard Glotin, S.J., in the little booklet, "SIGN OF SALVATION, The Sacred Heart of Jesus," makes a compelling case for the scriptural centrality of the devotion in the whole history of salvation. He begins by pointing out that Pope John Paul II, in his first encyclical, *The Redeemer of Man*, "defined the mystery of man in reference to the mystery of the Heart of Christ."

Dealing with Christian images, he points out the earliest ones: the Good Shepherd saving the lamb, Daniel saved from the lions, Jonah saved from the ocean, Moses striking the rock to give saving

water: all representing Christian salvation from death. Next to be put
into use in the historical series comes the cross. Soon after, artists
begin to show it together with the mystic rock on which stands the
victorious lamb and from which originate the four rivers of paradise.
The crowning point of this progression of images is reached in the
thirteenth century. From that period comes "the first crucifix in a
Roman apse which has come down to us." Jesus appears there as the
fruit of the tree of life. In subsequent art, a woman, image of the
Church, is sometimes seen holding up a chalice to collect the life-giving streams from his side.

Further developing his treatment of this symbolism, Fr. Glotin
concludes that the whole Gospel of John, which is the Gospel of liturgical signs, *is structured to bring out the pierced side as THE sign
of salvation.* **"The pierced Heart is a symbolic summary of the
paschal mystery."**

Fr. Karl Rahner's affirmative views of the Heart of Jesus devotion are also summarized in "Symbols, Devotions and Jesuits" (pp.
39-55). In his doctoral dissertation, "From the Side of Christ," he
studied the pre-history of the devotion, and finds it goes back to the
biblical symbolism of Christ's pierced side in John. He engages in a
profound analysis of primary words, the theology of symbols, and
Christological observations, and from these he draws his conclusions.
He observes, for instance, that the primary word, heart, doesn't originate with anatomists but with human experience. Found in all languages, it remains rooted in the body organ, but ranges out to mean
also the whole person and the ungraspable mystery of human existence. Awake and asleep, it surges up as an archetype. The meaning
of the devotion must be sought within this framework of mystery
analyzed ontologically and theologically.

People need these key focal words and symbols to help them
grasp their religion. Rahner finds in the Heart of Jesus devotion a way
for believers to focus on the Savior's deeds of love.

Rahner envisions the devotion as able to channel grace for the
priest of the future. The failings he perceived among modern priests
included activism, aridity of heart, withering of contemplation, and
a tendency to expect remedies by institutional change.

He predicted that the priests of tomorrow will bear witness through the vigor of their own experience of God. Human hearts pierced by the evils of the times will be the ones called to priesthood. With hearts like the Pierced One, they will be able to lead the flocks to their Fountain of Life.

He observes that the devotion has taken many forms, but that some people have been repelled by the sentimentality of certain of its artwork, and the cloying effusiveness of some of its prayers. One of the needed improvements is to direct the devotion's energy by Christ's teaching in Matthew 25: "Whatever you did for one of these least brothers of mine you did for me." Reparation must build the kingdom by working with Christ, loving his people with him, and serving them with him. This requires creative fidelity to the meaning of the devotion if it is to flourish today.

To these theological witnesses it is suitable to add the testimony of one who attests from experience to the value of the Apostleship of Prayer and the devotion to the Heart of Jesus in any situation, including the worst conditions imaginable. That testimony is found in explicit form in the life and writings of the servant of God, Father Walter J. Ciszek, S.J. His book, *He Leadeth Me*, is a case history of living the life of the Apostleship of Prayer and the Morning Offering through thick and thin—even in dread Lubianka, one of the places in the Soviet Union where he was imprisoned.

Fr. Ciszek experienced day after day that saying and living the Morning Offering helped him see the profound truth about God's will for his life. Offering his own sacrifices with the sacrifice of the Mass gave them meaning. He found out that hopelessness came from injecting too much of self into life. It was his experience that we worry too much about what we can or cannot do, but *we can do God's will*, and doing that restores hope.

The daily offering helped him discover that God's will is not hidden away somewhere. The situations he found himself in were God's will for him for the present. Seeing this was a "conversion" that transformed his life.

He muses on the Morning Offering: "Offering back to God each morning all the joys, works and sufferings of that day: But those are abstract words. What it means, in practice, is spelled out as always by the poor old body."

He wrote that "Redemption... consists in doing the will of God, no more and no less." It was this spirit of offering everything to God according to God's will, as the Morning Offering does, that gave profound meaning to his days of imprisonment and slave labor in Russia. He found he was working with God the Creator and Christ the Carpenter in his labor camp work. His daily offering was a selfless prayer. He was keenly aware of the courageous Christians suffering in the labor camp with him. He wrote, "Their faith, their courage, inspire me to offer up all my actions and works and sufferings of each day to the work of spreading the kingdom of God each day."

He shared what he believed. He gave a retreat to fellow prisoners, and taught them that their life, work and suffering had meaning in God's providence. "So we taught them the Morning Offering to dedicate to God all the prayers, works, joys and sufferings of each day in conformity to his will—as a means of winning grace for others, especially for their families and friends."

"The Morning Offering," he wrote, "is still one of the best practices of prayer." What greater proof do we need than that it worked in Russian prison camps for himself and those he taught?

Let there be added one final witness, a witness to the power of the Apostleship of Prayer at work in a great and vast country: The newsletter from the International Office of the Apostleship of Prayer, Rome, dated April, 1992, reports that Archbishop Luciano Mendes, President of the Brazilian bishops' conference, said it is largely due to the Apostleship of Prayer that Brazil has remained a Catholic country.

The evidence has been presented. It is time to draw from it the conclusion to our question, *Are the Apostleship of Prayer and devotion to the Heart of Jesus important for the 21st century of the Christian era?* The answer must be affirmative beyond doubt. What can serve Christians better than this spirituality which unites each one so tenderly and personally with God's own Son in his human and divine person? What is better than this spirituality of profound reverence and profound familiarity with God?

What can improve this commitment to do God's will in everything and acceptance of it in everything every day? What is better than uniting all I am and do daily with Christ my Redeemer, true God and true Man? And, mindful "that Christ died for our sins" (1 Cor 15:3), uniting it with him "in the Holy Sacrifice of the Mass throughout the world"? And thus being reminded daily by that phrase in the Morning Offering that "the Eucharist is above all else a sacrifice" as Pope John Paul II insisted in *Dominicae Cenae* (#9). And through offering him my "prayers, works, joys and sufferings of this day," accepting all as God wills; and tenderly making a reparation of love to his Heart in a most selfless way, offering myself with him suffering, for his selfsame purpose, "in my flesh... filling up what is lacking in the sufferings of Christ on behalf of his body which is the Church..." (Col 1:24).

And what can I do more praiseworthy than be with him at the Holy Sacrifice daily if I can be, and at least there on the paten with him through my Daily Offering if I cannot? What can give greater meaning to my life than this way of life in which I obey the Father's will? How better return to his beloved Son love for love, sacrifice for sacrifice, and service for service? How better offer everything I do to be used by him to build the civilization of love, the kingdom of his Heart in which the Gospel call will go out loud and clear, summoning everyone to eternal life with him through baptism and the Eucharist and union with his body the Church?

How can I better unite with the Church in need than in this way, and by remembering in my Daily Offering the intentions the Holy Father has given us for the Church each month? And offering all of this to his pierced Heart through the Immaculate Heart of Mary, the Heart spiritually pierced when she stood at the foot of his cross and saw the lance flash. How better draw closer to her, the most faithful, selfless, beloved, zealous, lovable, imitable disciple and comrade he has ever had and the world will ever see?

Would not anyone who understands these things be hard pressed to name a spirituality tailored for everyone that is more suited for the twenty-first century of the Christian era?

That, then, is why this new book of homilies on the Heart of Jesus and the Apostleship of Prayer has been published.

Chapter One

HIS HEART REVEALED

Homilies for
THE SOLEMNITY OF THE SACRED HEART
AND OTHER SUITABLE OCCASIONS

1. The Love that Evangelizes
2. Becoming a Disciple Jesus Loves
3. The Celebration of Love

Bad homilies offer theories
Good homilies offer practices

"A" — Solemnity of the Sacred Heart   Dt 7:6-11
1 Jn 4:7-16
Mt 11:25-30

THE LOVE THAT EVANGELIZES

HOMILETIC REALIZATIONS

Day after day we priests are so conscious that our lives are laden with important labors which give meaning to our faith and our commitment to Jesus that we can underestimate the indispensable need others have for a continuous felt devotion to Jesus. We can forget that many persons who are not moved by their feelings for Jesus are not moved to labor for him. But Jesus himself, understanding affairs so much better than we, appeals to his people to gather close enough to feel the beat of his Heart's love for them, and to respond to his call to enlist in his service of love.

Our task today is to stir hearts with the sense of Jesus's love for them, so they will respond with true devotion: the readiness to do God's will. His will includes the call to share in the work of proclaiming the Gospel with life and limb, as the Daily Offering of the Apostleship of Prayer has us promise to do.

To preach with any passion on this Solemnity we need to realize with our own hearts that the Feast deals with the heart of our faith: that the God-Man loves us, that he calls us to love in return, and that the returned love must be like his, a praying, serving love, the kind of love which lies behind the New Evangelization the Church stresses in this age.

THE LOVE THAT EVANGELIZES

"Take my yoke upon your shoulders and learn from me, for I am gentle and humble of heart." In that heartwarming personal invitation, Jesus calls to each one of us today. What if he had given that invitation to only a few chosen ones? Wouldn't we feel bad not to be in their number? But thanks be to God on this great Solemnity of his Heart that it is not so! He has extended this personal invitation to all who labor and are burdened, and I think that everyone who is working to live the faith can claim to be among that number.

But with the invitation comes the task of understanding it so we can respond with devotion. What is our Divine Lord asking us to do when he tells us to come to know his Sacred Heart and shoulder his yoke? I will try to bring out his meaning by making a comparison between nuclear energy and the Morning Offering. Hopefully you know that the Morning Offering is the prayer by which millions of us who are members of the Apostleship of Prayer daily consecrate ourselves and our day to the Heart of Jesus.

Now the comparison. For years scientists have been attempting to design an invisible magnetic bottle capable of containing the fiery plasma released in the type of reaction used in a nuclear bomb. Success would mean the ability to control a sun-like source of unlimited energy here on earth, and put it to work not at an explosive rate, but at any pace we want, when and as we wish, whether to power a car or fly a plane.

Years ago, the founders of the Apostleship of Prayer, the League of the Heart of Jesus, succeeded in something similar in the spiritual order. They designed the Morning Offering to release the unlimited divine energy of the love of the Heart of the Son of God— to release it into our hearts every morning of our lives by committing ourselves to unbounded daily love of our Savior and God. Then our days and nights burn bright with love and service of him and his.

That is what it means to take his yoke upon us—the yoke of carrying out the Mission of Love which his Father gave him and gives us through him.

It is this daily love of God that inspires us to live the Gospel of love. The daily consecration to the Heart of Love is a daily stimulus to act on our call to love and serve one another. Only when we are on fire with the love of the God-Man will we constantly love and serve well. That is why Jesus asked Peter, "Do you love me?", and heard his *yes* before he charged him with a Shepherd's care of his Church. Let us too give him our *yes* today when we receive him in Holy Communion.

Jesus commissioned St. Margaret Mary to bring about this Feast of his Sacred Heart in the whole Church. He asked expressly that this Feast be celebrated each year on the Friday after the Feast of His Body and Blood. Surely he asked for the connection between the two Feasts to convince us that we can scale the heights of devotion for him only by uniting ourselves to his Heart in receiving him body and blood, soul and divinity.

All of the prayers and acts of love Jesus asks of us are acts of evangelization because they help bring Jesus to others and others to Jesus. They are acts of sharing his yoke of atonement for sinners. St. Margaret Mary knew this. She said: "It seems to me that our Lord's earnest desire to have his Sacred Heart honored in a special way is directed toward the effects of redemption in our souls. For the Sacred Heart is an inexhaustible fountain and its sole desire is to pour itself out into the hearts of the humble so as to free them and prepare them to lead lives according to his good pleasure" (*Office*, Oct. 16).

Don't think of Jesus as a lover pining in a corner. He is a strong lover so ardent of heart he calls to us in lowly ways lesser lovers are too proud to adopt. He does it in order to save even the most ungrateful sinner from an eternity without love—that is, from hell.

Sharing Jesus's yoke makes evangelization our mission. The prayers and readings today overflow with the fire of God's love and our responding love. Jesus shares everything with us: his Father, his Heart, his Mother, his mission. He shared that mission with us at our baptism and calls us to it today: "Take my yoke upon your shoulders."

His is the mission of revealing to the little ones the love of God the Father who sent him, the Father's Son, as an offering for our sins.

Jesus charges us to share the lifelong mission he had of evangelizing by everything we are, say and do, but especially by loving him more ardently, and serving him more generously in all his members. He gave us the joy of calling all creation to share our God of love, Father, Son, and Holy Spirit.

Proclaim the Good News! As St. John teaches us in today's second reading, God loved us first. God goes on loving us first, sinners
and all. Everyone can join us in turning from sin to God and to love,
and be saved. Let the whole world hear the Good News from us! Let
us pray and live the Daily Offering joined to the Heart of our Savior.
Our works may reach only to those nearby, but our prayers will reach
to the ends of the earth.

OUTLINE:

I. An invitation and a task: Understand & Respond!
   * "Take my yoke upon you... humble of heart."
   * Thank God that his invitation includes us. But what is asked?
   * A Comparison: magnetic bottle and the Morning Offering.
   * Apostleship of Prayer/League Founders succeeded spiritually:
      Morning Offering.
   * Channels power to go on mission with Jesus.
   * It consecrates us daily to share yoke/mission from Father.

II. Daily love of God inspires us to live the Gospel of love:
   * Daily Consecration keeps love's fire alive.
   * Only love's fire keeps us faithful: why Jesus asked Peter.... Let
      us say YES today in Holy Communion.
   * Jesus asked St. Margaret Mary for this Feast after Corpus
      Christi—because devotion to his Heart is greatest in Commun-
      ion.
   * St. Margaret Mary: his aim is the salvation of souls.

III. Sharing Jesus's yoke makes Evangelization our mission.
   * Prayers/Readings today: fire of God's love.
   * Jesus shares everything with us....
   * Even his mission of revealing the Father's love to little ones.
   * He charges us with his yoke, his mission.
   * If we pray/live Daily Offering joined to his Heart, our works
      will reach at least those nearby, but our prayers will reach to
      the ends of the earth.

"B" — Solemnity of the Sacred Heart   Hos 11:1, 3-4, 8-9
                                             Eph 3:8-12, 14-19
                                             Jn 19:31-37

BECOMING A DISCIPLE JESUS LOVES

HOMILETIC REALIZATIONS

The historical and eschatological cry, "We would like to see Jesus" (Jn 12:21), infused in every heart by the Holy Spirit, is addressed to bishops as successors of the Apostles, and the response is also entrusted to us priests as episcopal assistants. If that cry is not heard clearly from the faithful today, one reason is that a sense of who Jesus is for them has been clouded over by the events and concerns of our times.

That leaves us with the urgent task of awakening many to the cry suffocated within their hearts. And to carry out that task we need all the help we can get.

Every trade and profession has its trade secrets and shortcuts for doing the expected job. The specialty of teaching the spiritual life, and teaching Christianity itself, is no exception to this rule.

Any time, then, that we teachers of the spiritual life can give a follower of Christ a simple and appealing means to better realize and respond to Jesus's personal love for him or her, we have an opportunity it would be derelict to neglect.

The readings today, especially from the Gospel of John, give us an outstanding opportunity to include such help in today's homily, and the homily that follows is devoted to executing this opportune task.

BECOMING A DISCIPLE JESUS LOVES

"One of the soldiers thrust a lance into his side, and... blood and water flowed out."

Dear brothers and sisters in Christ, on hearing these dread and solemn words, let us stir up in ourselves the grateful impulse to take them into our heart, lest we be, in the words of Shakespeare, a "marble-hearted fiend." How better do that than by seeing the flashing lance with Mary's eyes, seeing it pierce that sacred side, and feeling it with her loving Heart, feeling the pain of the lance plunging into her and us by plunging into him. If we know as we ought that it is our sins that have led him to bear this fate, we will be stirred to do no less.

But there are riches of love and grace to be drawn for a lifetime from this profound event. So we let this lance pierce our mind as well by looking further into the significance of the pierced side. The way St. John's Gospel records the piercing of Jesus' side makes us ask questions: Why did two prophets of old foretell it? Why is it so important that John adds his own prophetic word by insisting he is an eyewitness to the ancient prophecy's fulfillment?

The Fathers of the Church answer us: from the pierced side come forth the water symbolic of our baptism, and the blood of our Eucharistic drink. St. Augustine says of the pierced side, "There the purse which held our price was opened, for when the soldier's spear opened his side, the price of the whole world flowed forth."[1] In brief, the piercing of Jesus' side can be called not just a sign of salvation but the sign of salvation.

St. John's witness has further meaning for each of us individually. John, who knew he was the disciple Jesus loved, is teaching us how to learn about ourselves what he knew about himself. When he recalls Zechariah's prophecy, "They will look upon him whom they have pierced," he leads us to look up the prophecy and learn there is more: "and they shall mourn over him as one mourns for an only son." John is teaching us to meditate on that pierced side and, drawn by love, boldly enter the pierced Heart within. There we discover what he, John, knew, and what St. Paul learned: I am a disciple of Jesus the Son of God "who loved me and delivered himself

---

[1] Sermon 329, used as 2nd rdg., Common of One Martyr, *Office* vol. III, p. 1713.

up for me" (Gal 2:20). And so, in quoting Zechariah's prophecy, "They shall look on him whom they have pierced," John is prophesying **about us.**

Once we learn this, each of us can take possession of our truest, most God-given identity: "I am a disciple Jesus loves." And then with joy we become the evangelizers and witnesses Jesus appointed us to be. We become committed to live in such a way that our very lives proclaim to all that "You, like me, can be a disciple Jesus loves! Enter that pierced side in prayer and Holy Communion, find his love for you, and be set on fire to return it."

Jesus himself calls those of us who are lovers of his Sacred Heart to certain spiritual practices. Sixteen centuries after John, Jesus appeared to St. Margaret Mary, and appointed her to spread the call to return his love. He called in particular for this Solemnity of His Sacred Heart, for First Friday Communions of reparation, and for the Holy Hour.

Zealous priests founded and spread the Apostleship of Prayer to evangelize the world by fidelity to the Heart of Jesus. This "great family of prayer," in the words of Pope Paul VI, say a Daily Offering in which they offer themselves and their day to Jesus in union with his Holy Sacrifice of the Mass, for Jesus' intentions and for those of his Vicar on earth, the Holy Father.

You can join us, whom Pope John Paul II called "this immense communion of prayer," in 1994, the 150th anniversary of the Apostleship of Prayer. He urged us on in the work of "building up both the universal Church and the local churches." Promise Jesus you will make the Daily Offering, and live it in the spirit of reparation that undoes sin in the world, and say at least a decade of Our Lady's Rosary. Go to work with him to bring all into the civilization of love, the Kingdom of the Heart of Christ!

Like God in the first reading, we renounce anger and revenge, and open our hearts even to the most sinful. Like the Psalmist, we draw and drink the water of love from the well of Jesus' open side. Unselfishly, we call all to drink. Like Paul in the second reading, we marvel at God's love. Emboldened by it we "draw near to God and speak to him confidently" in prayer. Making our home in Jesus'

Heart, and opening our heart and home to others, we become living Gospels of the Heart of the Son of God.

HOMILY OUTLINE

* "One of the soldiers thrust a lance...."
* Open your hearts to these words... enter Mary's Heart....
* Feel the pain, aware that it was our sins that thrust the lance.
I. **To reap the riches here we let the lance pierce our minds as well:** two questions: Why the old and new prophecies?
    * Answer of Fathers of the Church; St. Augustine's dictum.
II. **St. John's witness has meaning for each of us individually:**
    * He sends us to learn more from Zechariah.
    * We learn to meditate, to enter the wound, the Heart.
    * We learn about ourselves what John knew, what Paul learned.
    * The joy in our identity and the mission it gives us....
III. **The practices to which Jesus himself calls us:**
    * St. Margaret Mary: on this Feast; First Fridays; Holy Hour.
    * Founding and purpose of the Apostleship of Prayer.
    * Join us: unite with Jesus to bring the Kingdom of love.
    * We imitate God in Reading One, Psalmist in Two, Paul in Three.
    * In Jesus's Heart we open our hearts, become living Gospels of the Heart of the Son of God.

"C" — Solemnity of the Sacred Heart   Ezk 34:11-16
                                                                            Rm 5:5-11
                                                                            Lk 15:3-7

THE CELEBRATION OF LOVE

HOMILETIC REALIZATIONS

The family, the Church, and the family of mankind lean on one another. Families desperately need help, the Church needs to help and needs the help of families, and the family of mankind is helpless without the health and help of both. This season of the Sacred Heart is a favorable time to draw individuals and families to the only Heart formed in families divine and human. Meditation on this fact of faith provides insights into right family living, and wins the grace to live what we learn.

Families live by love, or fail as families. How better help them than by drawing them to the Heart of Love, there to drink of love at the Fountain of living water through prayer and the reception of the sacrament of the Real Presence?

SUGGESTED PENITENTIAL RITE:

To prepare ourselves to celebrate this sacred mystery of Christ lovingly offering himself on Calvary for the forgiveness of our sins, let us call to mind our wrongdoing, and pray to be washed in the rivers of living water streaming from his pierced side.

* For what we have done in the past, or failed to do, that wounded the Heart of Jesus and damaged his kingdom of love, LORD HAVE MERCY....
* For what we are doing in the present, or failing to do, that wounds the Heart of Jesus and damages his kingdom of love, CHRIST HAVE MERCY....

* For the grace not to do anything in the future, by commission or omission, that would wound the Heart of Jesus and damage his kingdom of love, LORD HAVE MERCY....

THE CELEBRATION OF LOVE

"Rejoice with me because I have found my lost sheep."
Today we are called to celebrate God's love. We celebrate the happiness of knowing that God loves us his human family. Like a proud child babbling about an admired father, we're called to boast of God's love for us.

The Almighty has in truth loved us, loved us so much that he sent his only Son to shed his blood for us even when we were rebels by sin. All the more should we celebrate now that we are making earnest efforts to return his love.

Listen again to the first sentence from that first reading, the one from Ezekiel: "Thus says the Lord God: I myself will look after and tend my *family*. As a shepherd tends his flock when he finds himself among his scattered sheep, so will I tend my *family*. I will rescue them...." Did you notice that in two places I replaced the word *sheep* with the word *family*?

I'm sure you know I made the substitution to bring out the parable's deeper meaning. Who are God's sheep except the whole human family, and then, more intimately, the family of his Church and the domestic family born of each Christian marriage?

We help the Good Shepherd to search, find and celebrate each lost sheep found. In today's Gospel we find the Good Shepherd, Heart burning with love, out searching for a lost member of his family. When he finds the lost one he comes home rejoicing and calling for a celebration. Let's celebrate for his sake, and for our own, and for everyone he has found. Love has found us, and taken us into the very Heart of God. We have found the home where we belong, in the Heart of Love. Let us celebrate!

But in many dark and wild and dangerous places lost sheep still wander. Must we not give the Good Shepherd joy by going out to find them, recognize him in them, and bring them to him? By sinning we once strayed and wounded our Good Shepherd's Heart; the least we can do is make amends by rescuing other strays and carrying them to him on our shoulders through our prayers and penance and good works.

The Apostleship of Prayer, the League of the Heart of Jesus, was founded to make us more faithful searchers of lost souls. Each day that we say and live the Daily Offering for the intentions of the Heart of Jesus, we accompany him that day in searching for lost sheep and finding them. We seek sheep lost not only to sin, but to poverty, degradation, alienation, and any injustice. Let us recognize them and go to their help as far as we can. But never let us neglect those suffering from the worst alienation of all, the alienation from God. Ought we not to want most of all for others what we want most of all for ourselves, love of God given and received forever?

Each time our prayers or deeds reconcile members of a family, a parish, or a community, we return lost sheep to Christ, and to the security of his flock.

How celebrate love except by loving? Let us make this a day of loving, first showing love to Christ in prayer and Eucharist, then to family and friends and strangers by thoughtful words and ways. In chapter seven of John's Gospel, Jesus invites us to come and drink of the rivers of living water of the Holy Spirit. These rivers flow from his pierced side, his Sacred Heart, to parched lips of all ages. These are the rivers of life and grace, especially the river of his Eucharistic blood in Holy Communion. Let our love and joy and celebration overflow above all in Holy Communion, the crowning gift of God, the gift of himself, body and blood, soul and divinity.

Eternal God, we celebrate Your love today. We celebrate it proudly, gratefully, full of eager desire to return to you all the love we can, by the power of the Holy Spirit, through the Immaculate Heart of Mary, to the Sacred Heart of Jesus, and with him and in him to you, eternal Father of our Lord Jesus Christ. Amen.

HOMILY OUTLINE:

* "Rejoice with me...."

I. Today, we are called to celebrate God's love for his human family:
   * Like a child, proud, babbling about an admired father....
   * Truly God has loved us... shed his blood for us rebels.
   * We celebrate the more now that we're returning his love.
   * First sentence of first reading: replace **Sheep** with **Family**.
   * Did you notice the substitution? We: God's family: human family, Church family, domestic family.

II. We help Jesus search, find and celebrate:
   * See him searching in today's Gospel, Heart burning with love.
   * Finding, he comes rejoicing; let's celebrate for his sake, for our own, for everyone he has found.
   * Love has found us, we've found home... the Heart of Love.
   * But lost sheep still wander. Let's help find them....
   * We once wounded our Good Shepherd's Heart; let us make amends by rescuing other strays....
   * The Apostleship of Prayer & Daily Offering: make us better rescuers. Each day we say/live the Daily Offering we join the Good Shepherd searching.
   * Each time we reconcile... we return a lost sheep.
   * We seek sheep lost to sin or to poverty, degradation, etc.

III. How celebrate love except by loving?
   * This: a day of loving: Christ in prayer and Eucharist; family, friends, strangers: by thoughtful words and ways.
   * Jesus invites us to drink... Holy Spirit... from his pierced side: parched lips of all ages... especially via blood of Holy Communion.
   * *Eternal God, we celebrate Your love today, celebrate it proudly, gratefully, and full of eager desire to return to you all the love we can, by the power of the Holy Spirit, through the Immaculate Heart of Mary, to the Sacred Heart of Jesus, and with him and in him to you, eternal Father of our Lord Jesus Christ. Amen.*

Chapter Two

HIS MOTHER'S HEART

Homilies on
THE IMMACULATE HEART OF MARY
1. The Immaculate Heart Revealed
2. Mary's Instructive Heart
3. Mary's Willpower

His only Son He sent to exile in the womb,
Till Mary as a fountain brought Him forth
A torrent of Love bringing flood time
To the delta of the World

Saturday after the Solemnity of the Sacred Heart: Is 7:11-15 (optional)
Immaculate Heart of Mary   Lk 2:41-51

THE IMMACULATE HEART REVEALED

HOMILETIC REALIZATIONS

Before we go deep into doctrine and theology in matters of the heart, it is far more profitable to elicit from hearing hearts before us thoughts and moods too deep for words. The assigned Gospel reading for the memorial of the Immaculate Heart of Mary is a powerful invitation to pursue this truth. The loss in the Temple is an inexplicable event that is a true mystery of faith, illumined only as such mysteries are, by meditative prayer walking the paths of love and faith and the feelings of the heart.

We had best not attempt to preach on this Gospel pericope without first taking it prayerfully to Mary and to her Spouse the Holy Spirit for light and for devotion. The homily that follows was not written without the attempt to proceed in this fashion, and almost certainly will not be helpful to a homilist who does not approach it in the same Spirit. Things of love are accessible only to lovers.

THE IMMACULATE HEART REVEALED

"Son, why have you done this to us?"

Everything about Mary in this deeply moving event calls to mind the lovely little girl spotted in an airport with the words emblazoned across her blouse, "Made for love." On entering Mary's Heart as she suffers through these three days, we find her living out her love as memory, as present devotion, and as inexpressible longing.

Three days she walks the ways of searching. What an eternity of time for memories to flood in! Memories of an angel, a pregnancy, a birth; memories of Isaiah's words: "The Virgin shall be with child, and shall bear a son, and shall name him Immanuel"; memories of nursing her Child with a love never known before. Still earlier memories: kneeling on cold earth ceaselessly pleading heaven to send his Messiah, send him to the womb of some worthy virgin somewhere among her people. Send their Savior!

Memories of Elizabeth, prophet, aware of the Child in her womb, though no telltale signs informed her. Memories of her fiancé Joseph's shock as signs of pregnancy appeared. Memories of his first stirrings in her womb, his Savior's Heart beating there beneath her own pulsing Heart, stirrings that awakened wondrous longing to see him and feel him in her arms.

Now love present sweeps all past thoughts away. "Where can he be?" she and Joseph ask each other, and wrack their brains searching out avenues to explore. If you think the valiant woman doesn't weep, look again and see tears come unbidden; see a young Mother, body and soul immaculate and fair, still glistening from the touch of God's creative hand, a frail young woman with a Son, Heart full of all the treasured memories of a mother's heart and a mother's grief.

The more they search, the more anxiety and longing flood in, until she cries to the Father, a living Song of Songs, "Have you seen him whom my heart loves?"

Now they come to the Temple, and Lo! he bursts upon their sight, untroubled and engaged in calm words as though the world were not all turmoil for three long days! "Son, why have you done this to us?" The words burst out unbidden. How could you, who are more myself than I, you, Life drawn from my flesh and my womb, sharer of my joys and sorrows and all else—how be so unconcerned when we have been so long lost to one another!

"Son, why have you done this to us?" Can we, too, not offer you an answer to your question, Mary our Mother? Is it not so that you will come to understand us, your sinful children? Is it not so that you will learn to grieve with us when we lose our Savior by neglect of prayer, and worse, by sin? Is it not to move your Heart to pray for us to escape our hells of loneliness and find reunion with our Lord and Savior?

Is it not so that your life may teach us what we too must learn? That the Lord's ways are mysterious and who can trace their hidden pattern until they are consummated? That we must learn from you to trust, learn to say: "He who has not spared his own Son, but has delivered him up for us, how can it be that with him we have not received all things?" (Rm 8:32). That though we are not able to suppress all fear and anxiety and doubt and dread, these too, O Lord, are human things you use to bring us the more to you, for "We know that all things work for good for those who love God" (Rm 8:28).

Suffering can seem so useless in us, but you, our Virgin Mother, teach us that it serves the same purpose it did in you. As an oyster covers an irritant within its shell with self-protective layers until a pearl forms, you learned to enclose your sufferings in abandonment to divine providence, and in adoration of the wisdom of God that rules the world. And so you produced your life of faithfulness, the Pearl of Great Price so loved and admired by the whole world that all generations will call you blessed.

And so, instructed by your Immaculate Heart, O Virgin Mother of God, we too keep these things in our hearts. And as you came at length, through prayer and life, to understand Jesus's answer to your question, teach us to understand it through our prayer and our lives, so we may become one heart with your Heart and his Heart divine.

Saturday after the Solemnity of the Sacred Heart: 2 Cor 5:14-21 (optional)
Immaculate Heart of Mary   Lk 2:41-51

MARY'S INSTRUCTIVE HEART

HOMILETIC REALIZATIONS

In the Office for the Immaculate Conception, we find St. Anselm saying to Mary in the second reading: "Truly the Lord is with you, to whom the Lord granted that all nature should owe as much to you as to himself."

Who can really appreciate how much we owe Mary? In her Son she has given us the Life by which we live, and by which we love in accord with the new commandment he gave us, and gave us power to obey.

Christian gratitude to our Mother Mary should inspire all of us to a love that has no bounds. We preachers have a needed role in the way believers come to realize that. The memorial of the Immaculate Heart of Mary is a privileged opportunity to engage in the effort to sing her praises in a way to stir hearts and win them to our Lady.

The memorial of the Immaculate Heart of Mary has assigned to it the Gospel reading listed above; the second reading is the reading for the day, which is the case with the one given above when the memorial falls on the Saturday of the tenth week of ordinary time. But it is licit to choose a first reading from the Common of the Blessed Virgin Mary, or elsewhere, to help convey the truths and lessons most needed.

MARY'S INSTRUCTIVE HEART

"His Mother kept all these things in her Heart"

If the Gospels are letters from home, from God our Father, their words are to be kept in our hearts to be dwelt on always. When they are some of God's rare words about Mary, all the more do we hold them dear, and try to penetrate to their sweet essence. And on this day we celebrate Mary's Immaculate Heart, it is no accident the passage the Church selected for us relates a family affair. For nothing more than family life with its joys and sorrows tests and reveals the human heart. But I should correct that: nothing reveals the human heart more than family life except our life with God; and God too is present in this passage, in the person of Mary's young Son, and the work he is doing.

Central to this event are two questions, one by Jesus and one by Mary, and to be instructed by the event we have to be alert to how many answers questions can give. The different ways questions are posed tell us much about another—or ourselves. There is the trusting question, and the doubting question, and the question which in effect is a statement. "Why does God allow all this suffering?" can be an honest question in search of an answer, or a way of expressing one's shaken faith, or an atheist's way of implying that God doesn't exist.

But to appreciate Mary's question, we need to know first that at that time the Holy Land was an occupied country. Jerusalem would have its contingent of Roman soldiers making themselves obnoxiously evident to suppress the ideas of violence and rebellion in the hearts of Jewish freedom fighters who might be lurking anywhere. The insurrection of Judas the Galilean, the false Messiah, may have been going on at the time, which by the best scholarly estimate was about the year 6 A.D.

This explains better why, when Jesus' parents saw their twelve-year-old Son sitting calmly in the Temple, after they had spent three very anxious days searching for him, "they were astonished." He was no baby! How could he be so thoughtless! How could he not be anxious for them, knowing how worried they would be!

And so her question, poured out in a voice of suffering:

"Son, why have you done this to us?"

In all creation one could find no more feeling heart than the Heart of the boy to whom that Mother spoke. Enter that filial Heart and feel with him his compassion for his parents in their suffering.

How did Jesus understand that question? This Son knew that this Mother did not ask her question as a challenge or a doubt, but in a plea to be given understanding. And that was the way her question served for Joseph as well, as his silence made evident.

And so their Son answered with a question: "Did you not know that I must be in my Father's house?" Jesus' answer poses a problem, first, for translators. Mary and Joseph would know at once that it meant as well, "I must be about my Father's work," as the New American Bible indicates.

But even with both meanings before her, did Mary understand? Or did she have to keep his words in her heart and ponder them long before she really understood? We ought to remember here that the word "heart," in the devotion to the Hearts of Jesus and Mary, as well as in the whole Bible and in other literatures, has a profound and inexhaustible meaning. It is the beating heart ever at work laboring for the life of the body, and feeling and registering our deepest emotions. But it is also the sum total of our deepest thoughts and values; it is the word for those inexpressible inner depths where we really live, and where those we love are invited to live with us.

Face to face here with a grievous misunderstanding within a family, we need to learn from it the lesson that sometimes in our family fallouts there is literally *no one to blame!* There is mystery to life, there are limits to communications, there are events which cannot be explained beforehand.

Some people are "all thumbs" not only in their handling of objects, but in their handling of their human relationships, but that was not the case with the Holy Family. They are teaching us that even among the best families there can be stress, especially at a time when one member of the family is obeying conscience or some other call from God, like a vocation, as Jesus was obeying his Father. So Mary "kept all these things in her heart." That is, she pondered them and prayed over them.

What did Mary learn in her pondering and praying over this event and the words of her Son? Perhaps she learned from her silent husband the lesson, "Don't get upset. Get to pondering."

Certainly, she learned what all parents must, that God's claims precede their own, and the more faithful their children, the more this will be experienced. And in the case of Joseph and Mary's Son, the claim was most pressing and profound, since he was the eternal Son of God who became their Son twelve years earlier.

Almost certainly, another profound lesson she began to learn was the one the Christian people have been learning for two millennia: that the life of her Son penetrates and gives insight into the mystery of suffering. Pope John Paul II has expressed with profundity what the Church has learned from the life of Jesus: "Suffering is in the world to release love."

The three days of separation and the suffering until she found her boy only made her realize the more the gift God had given her, and increased her love for him and her gratitude to the Father. It also prepared her for their more terrible three days of separation as he lay in the tomb.

Now let us take a lesson. If despite all of today's needs and sufferings on every side moving us to compassion and the service of love we still sometimes resist that service, how much less would we love and serve if there were no needs and sufferings around us? How selfish and enclosed would we become? How unloving? Isn't it clear that we must walk with Jesus and carry the cross of the needs of others with Jesus if we are to be the members of Jesus?

Pope John Paul II has given us a beautiful phrase in describing the relationship of Jesus and Mary as "the alliance of the two hearts." In pondering the event in today's Gospel, Mary was no doubt helped to pattern her own Heart still more after the divine Heart of her Son, so that she too could say to us her children: "Come to me, all you who labor and are burdened, and I will give you rest.... Learn from me, for I am meek and humble of heart... and you will find rest for yourselves."

That is surely what Mary learned, and what we need to learn from Jesus and Mary for the sake of our families and friends, and above all, for the sake of laboring in the yoke of Jesus to advance the kingdom of God.

Saturday after the Solemnity of the   Si 24:1, 3-4, 8-12, 19-21 (optional)
Sacred Heart: Immaculate Heart of Mary   Lk 2:41-51

MARY'S WILLPOWER

HOMILETIC REALIZATIONS

Because a parent normally knows better than the child what is for its good, parents can love a child and yet act in ways that displease the child. But rationally, we can never claim we are loving God when we are pursuing paths which we do not know will please, or in fact know displease him. That truth was once a staple of Catholic teaching, but it seems to have been obscured by the new stress on love and freedom, as though the combination exonerates us from the lifelong task of seeking and finding and submitting to the will of God.

That even Mary had to struggle with this hard fact so contrary at times to personal happiness, is evident in today's Gospel reading. It provides a felicitous opportunity to bring to the fore the greater greatness of the Mother of God. Neither she nor her Son were beyond the laws of God; and far from being beyond the need to be at the service of God in life and career choice and all other things, they were at the service of nothing else unless it also advanced the service of God. If we can make that appealingly evident today, and evident that we are to do likewise, ours will be a blessed homily.

MARY'S WILLPOWER

"Son, why have you done this to us?"

This question of the Virgin Mary to her divine Son parallels her question to the Angel Gabriel. To Gabriel announcing that she was to be the Mother of the Son of God, she said, "How can this be since I have no relations with a man?"

The words of the angel thrust her into a struggle of faith. Should she believe him? How to reconcile motherhood with her virginal state? Now, the actions of her Son have thrown her into consternation. How to understand, and by understanding, humbly and graciously submit to such conduct by her young Son, not just now, but for all it portends for the future?

The struggle the angel precipitated and the struggle brought on by her Son's conduct show certain parallels and vast differences. The former struggle was of faith against humility; the latter, of obedience against self-will. Learning how Mary wins out in both cases will help us in our own struggles.

If I may make bold to say it, in the case of being called to be Mother of God, the honor was so great, what sane person would refuse, unless she could not see how it could be, or unless it be from some excessive humility?

Mary's question to Gabriel makes it clear that she is hesitating because she can't see how this call is compatible with her virginal state. How could she, a virgin, bear a child as the angel was saying?

But Mary's hesitation, according to St. Bernard, had roots in her humility as well. In meditating on the Annunciation, St. Bernard puts himself right into the event, and cries out to Mary about our plight. "Answer quickly, O Virgin," he says. "Why do you delay, why are you afraid? Believe, give praise, and receive. Let humility be bold, let modesty be confident. This is no time for virginal simplicity to forget prudence. In this matter alone, O prudent Virgin, do not fear to be presumptuous. Though modest silence is pleasing, dutiful speech is now more necessary. Open your heart to faith, O blessed Virgin, your lips to praise, your womb to the Creator." And Mary cries out, "Behold the handmaid of the Lord. Be it done to me according to your word" (*Divine Office*, December 20).

Now, three days of anguish brought on by her Son's conduct face Mary with a different struggle, one in which she has to win out, not over humility, but over pride and self-will. Now the issue is submission to God's purpose and plan even though she can't understand it. Now, the glory of radiant motherhood doesn't await her, but submission to suffering, deprivation, anguish and sorrows almost beyond bearing: submission to God's wisdom and God's will; submission to the same battle her Son would have to fight to subject his human will to the Father, the battle that reached its height in the Agony in the Garden.

Her Son answers her question: "Why were you looking for me? Did you not know that I must be in my Father's house?" The answer did not resolve the problem that led to Mary's question; it only provides her with a mystery to ponder: *Am I to cooperate with God's will and God's affairs even when I can't understand, even when my Immaculate Heart is pierced with sorrows, as Simeon foretold when we presented our Son in the Temple?*

Mary kept these things in her Heart, and was guided by the Holy Spirit to fuller understanding. St. Maximilian Kolbe, whom Pope John Paul II called the "Prophet of the civilization of love," wrote profoundly about Mary's relationship to the Holy Spirit, whose Spouse she was. He said the Spirit worked through her as his base of operations in the world. Only by the help of that same Holy Spirit, the Spirit of Truth, can we come to understand God's purposes well enough to submit our wills with cheerful good will.

After her Son, Mary is the greatest example and teacher of this sublime lesson. Mary was physically the Mother of God become Man, but Mary's greater greatness is that in all things without exception she turned her willpower over to God with gracious faith and loving submission. In all things, her life said, "Be it done unto me according to your word." This truth is confirmed by Jesus himself. When someone in the crowd praised her for bringing him forth, he said, "Rather, blessed is the one who hears the word of God and keeps it." Pondering this passage, St. Augustine says that "Mary certainly did the Father's will, and so it was a greater thing for her to have been Christ's disciple than to have been his Mother" (*Divine Office*, Presentation of Mary).

Jesus himself not only preached the word of God, but kept it. To his disciples he said, "My food is to do the will of the one who sent me and to finish his work" (Jn 4:34). In today's first reading, we learn the deeper meaning of his words. We find the Holy Spirit,

Wisdom, telling us that "You will remember me as sweeter than honey, better to have than the honeycomb. He who eats of me will hunger still, he who drinks of me will thirst for more. He who obeys me will not be put to shame; he who serves me will never fail." To those words, Mary's whole life as Spouse of the Holy Spirit adds "Amen!"

Mary learned from her Son's conduct and response that we don't always grasp God's ways but we must always adore them and gladly surrender our willpower to them to please him and work with his divine wisdom to advance the work of salvation and the civilization of love. That battle of submission was fought and won by Christ and by Mary. It is the same battle we must fight and win for the glory of God and our eternal glory with him.

Chapter Three

Homilies for the
SOLEMNITY OF CHRIST THE KING

"A" — Solemnity of Christ the King   Ezk 34:11-12, 15-17
                                                      1 Cor 15:20-26, 28
                                                      Mt 25:31-46

LIVING OUR BAPTISM AS
CHRIST OUR KING COMMANDS

HOMILETIC REALIZATIONS

A survey taken some years ago found that where parishioners are not allowed to forget the Last Things and the final consequences of their deeds, they live a more serious Christian life. Who was more aware of that than Christ? Who more powerfully described that scene of final judgment than he? It is a blessing for priest and people to have the advantage of his description in today's Gospel reading.

Today's homily, then, is a privileged opportunity to draw fruit from Christ's powerful revelation of the future. It is an excellent opportunity to inculcate some lasting habits that will support a more faithful living of each one's baptismal responsibilities. The homily that follows attempts just that, by inviting the faithful to take advantage of membership in the Apostleship of Prayer, with its practice of saying the Daily Offering.

The post-Vatican II Statutes of the Apostleship of Prayer make it evident that their very purpose is to assist the faithful to live their baptismal life more faithfully. "Through baptism," they assert, "all the faithful share in the function of Christ as priest, king, and prophet, and are appointed by God to apostolic activities in accord with their particular vocation. Within this universal apostolic vocation, the Apostleship of Prayer is a union of the faithful who, by their daily oblation unite themselves with the Eucharistic Sacrifice, in which the work of our redemption is continuously accomplished, and by this vital bond with Christ, upon which the fruitfulness of the apostolate depends, cooperate in the salvation of the world" (Part I).

When we build a homily on the foundation of Christ's word, connect it clearly with his sacramental system of Baptism and Eucharist, and lace it with the wisdom of a consecrated practice like saying and living the Daily Offering, we are truly evangelizing. We can be hopeful of not only reaping a rich harvest, but of helping the faithful to do the same throughout their lives, long after they have parted from us and gone their separate ways.

SUGGESTED PENITENTIAL RITE

Use of the Rite of Blessing and Sprinkling with Holy Water is appropriate.

LIVING OUR BAPTISM AS CHRIST OUR KING COMMANDS

"And these will go off to eternal punishment, but the righteous to eternal life."
   Today's Gospel illumines the true meaning of Christianity and of love.
   It also calls to mind the saying, "If you have anything to tell me of importance, for heaven's sake begin at the end!" It is **for heaven's sake** that our loving and merciful King and God begins at the end. He lifts us out of time and space to preview our final exam as human beings and as Christians.
   Throughout his teaching our Lord made it clear that love of God comes first, and that love of every person is inseparably bound up with love of God. "Amen, I say to you, whatever you did [and what you did not do] for one of these least brothers of mine, you did [or did not do] for me."
   Did you notice that in this Final Judgment Jesus mentions neither worship nor prayer? Why, except that worship and prayer form the roots of the tree of love of God, and if they are healthy, they will have made the tree of love bear fruit. So it is at the fruit that Jesus will look. For if faith without good works is dead, then certainly love without good works is dead!

Today I invite you to rekindle your baptismal call by joining the Apostleship of Prayer, the League of the Heart of Jesus.
Today's Gospel provides us with a powerful motive and the
best of guidance for such a rekindling! By the sacrament of baptism
we were freed from sin, reborn as children of God, configured to
Christ by an indelible character, and incorporated into his Church
(Canon 849). With the grace and example of Christ and the Saints,
and the help of the other sacraments, above all the Eucharistic
Sacrifice and Sacrament, we have mighty helps to live our life in
Christ faithfully enough to pass any final exam.

The Apostleship of Prayer is a further help to rekindling and
living our baptismal life. Its Statutes were rewritten after Vatican II
to sparkle with its updated teaching and spirit. Pope after Pope has
urged every Catholic to join. They have eloquently described how
the Apostleship draws us to love and serve the Heart of Jesus, from
which our baptism flowed and is nourished.

Pope Paul VI explained this admirably. He quoted Vatican II's
statement that "The Church, or, in other words, the kingdom of
Christ now present in mystery, grows visibly in the world through
the power of God. This inauguration and this growth are both symbolized by the blood and water which flowed from the open side of
the crucified Jesus" (*The Church*, #3). Then Pope Paul added, "For
the Church was born from the pierced Heart of Jesus and is nourished there" *(Investigabiles Divitias Christi*, 2/6/1965). From the
earliest days the Fathers of the Church taught the same thing when
they related the water from Jesus' side to our baptism, and saw in the
blood our Eucharistic nourishment.

By drinking from the Heart of Jesus both spiritually in prayer
and sacramentally in Holy Communion, we become imbued with the
fire of love and service which marked his life.

The Apostleship of Prayer, as Popes have pointed out repeatedly, inspires us not just to prayer. It inspires us to action, that is, to
the deeds of love and service to which our King is summoning us in
today's Gospel. That is why the Popes want every single Catholic,
even members of other apostolic organizations, to join it. Pope John

Paul II said that "The Apostleship of Prayer can bring a meaningful and concrete contribution to the diffusion, at all levels, of the great and consoling truth that all Christians can be intimately united to Christ the Redeemer by offering their own life to the Heart of Christ.... Thus will be accomplished Pius XII's hope that the 'Apostleship of Prayer... be so united to other pious Associations that it penetrates them like a breath of fresh air through which supernatural life and apostolic activity are ever renewed and strengthened'" (*L'Osservatore Romano* April 29, 1985, p. 5).

It is time now to invite you to join the Apostleship of Prayer, the League of the Heart of Jesus.

What do we have to do to be members? Please pick up the Daily Offering cards in the pews and pass them to one another as I answer that question. There are no meetings, no dues, no signatures, no obligation under sin. We need only say the Daily Offering each morning and live it as the love of Jesus our King draws us, and to say at least a decade of Our Lady's rosary. To join the League is to tell our Lord we love him, and love him enough to take this practical step because we want this daily help to faithfully living our baptismal promises of loving and serving him from the heart. If we sincerely make this offering to him each morning, the Holy Spirit will interiorly guide us to apply the spiritual, moral, and social teaching of the Church to our lives, so we can work with Jesus in building the civilization of love, the Kingdom of his Heart. Please join me in the Daily Offering now:

"O Jesus...."

I hope you noticed how that prayer communes tenderly with the Hearts of Jesus and Mary, and shows love of the Mass and the Eucharist and the Church, and concern for the Church's needs under the care of the Holy Father. That is why Pope Pius XII called the League a most effective school of divine love, and a way to lead families and society back to the love of God and neighbor (*Haurietis Aquas #188*).

I now invite you to join the Apostleship of Prayer, or to renew your membership. There is a plenary indulgence for joining, and even for renewing on this Feast Day, under the usual conditions. I'll first say the pledge so you can hear it, then repeat it phrase by phrase so you can say it after me.

LORD JESUS CHRIST MY KING—
I WISH TO BE A MEMBER—
OF THE APOSTLESHIP OF PRAYER—
THE LEAGUE OF YOUR SACRED HEART.—
I PROMISE TO SAY—
AND WITH YOUR HELP TO LIVE—
THE DAILY OFFERING.

Now if you wish to join, please stand and repeat the Pledge after me....

NOW I ADMIT YOU AS LIFELONG MEMBERS OF THE APOSTLESHIP OF PRAYER, THE LEAGUE OF THE SACRED HEART.

There are uncounted millions of us members around the world, helping the Church to build that Kingdom of loving service which our King describes in today's Gospel. May we be more than faithful enough to hear one day those longed-for words of our beloved King: "Come, you who are blessed by my Father. Inherit the kingdom prepared for you from the foundation of the world."

HOMILY OUTLINE:

    * "And these will go off to eternal punishment...."

   I. Today, Jesus illumines nature of Christianity, of love, and of our destiny.
    * Why Jesus speaks of good deeds, not of love, prayer, worship.
    * Love and prayer without good works are dead.

  II. Today: Rekindle your baptism by joining the Apostleship of Prayer, the League of the Heart of Jesus.
    * Motive and guidance from today's Gospel.
    * What baptism did for us: un-sinned; reborn; made Christlike, incorporated into Church: given sacraments and example of Saints.
    * The Apostleship of Prayer is a further help praised by Popes: it helps us serve the Heart of Jesus from which we were born, as the Gospel and Vatican II call us to do.

* Paul VI and Vatican II: Church, born/nourished from pierced side, grows still. We do too, and are fired up to love and serve.
* Popes want all to join Apostleship of Prayer because it's like today's Gospel call: joins intimately to Heart and service of Jesus and all his. Infuses prayer and the supernatural into all activities.

III. So now I invite you to join the Apostleship of Prayer
* The key duty of members.... Take up Daily Offering cards....
* We pledge in love to say and live the Daily Offering.
* The Holy Spirit will guide us to live it as Church teaches.
* Say the prayer with me now....
* The prayer communes with Hearts of Jesus and Mary, shows love of Mass, Holy Communion, Church, Holy Father, and concern for Church and world.
* Pius XII: The Apostleship of Prayer is a school of love, a way for families and society to return to love of God and neighbor.

IV. Invitation to Join: (Listen to pledge first, then I'll repeat)
LORD JESUS CHRIST MY KING—
I WISH TO BE A MEMBER—
OF THE APOSTLESHIP OF PRAYER—
THE LEAGUE OF YOUR SACRED HEART.—
I PROMISE TO SAY—
AND WITH YOUR HELP TO LIVE—
THE DAILY OFFERING.

To join, please stand and repeat....

I ADMIT YOU AS LIFELONG MEMBERS....

* We members number in scores of millions... we help to build the Kingdom of loving service which our King describes in today's Gospel. May we hear one day his longed-for words: "Come, you who are blessed by my Father. Inherit the kingdom prepared for you from the foundation of the world."

"B" — Solemnity of Christ the King   Dt 7:13-14
Rv 1:5-8
Jn 18:33-37

CONSECRATION TO THE HEART OF OUR KING

HOMILETIC REALIZATIONS

How can we give this homily in a way that will best help our people to know Christ their King more intimately, love him more ardently, and serve him more faithfully? That is the grace which St. Ignatius calls the exercitant to search for and beg for in the Kingdom Meditation of his *Spiritual Exercises.* That grace is also the ideal of the Apostleship of Prayer, which is based on the *Exercises.*

It is a call beyond words and feelings. As Ignatius says in his famous "Contemplation for Love," of which the Daily Offering is the counterpart in the Apostleship of Prayer, "Love ought to manifest itself in deeds rather than in words." The call of the King is a call to the service of love.

What if we can give a homily on this Feast of Christ the King that will lead people to adopt a lifelong practice that ties them more closely to the crux of the lived faith? By enrolling them in the Apostleship of Prayer, we can. Living this life consists in a conscious, daily act of personal commitment of love and service to Jesus in union with his Eucharist Sacrifice, and of sharing his yoke in daily life.

Jesus said, "Follow me." The call of our King is a call to action. So, too, is the Apostleship of Prayer. Today we have a perfect chance to enlist the troops in this apostleship, to serve their King for no less than a lifetime. What more than that can we do in any homily?

CONSECRATION TO THE HEART OF OUR KING

Is not Jesus Christ our King the first King in history who said, "My kingdom does not belong to this world"? Yet since then he has raised up Christian kings like St. Louis IX, King of France, who lived those words by devoting his life on earth to Christ and his people, as Jesus did and calls us all to do.

On this Feast of Christ the King, we can be helped to appreciate our privilege of having so great a king by reflecting on leadership. Then I will propose a help to fidelity to so good a King and Lord.

Many people today are dissatisfied with their leaders, even leaders they themselves elected. Over the ages people have wrestled with the problem of having worthy leaders. Plato said we'd have a good leader when a philosopher was king. A philosopher is a lover of truth. Our King has gone beyond Plato's recommendation. He loves the truth, and more. "I *am*" he said, "the truth." In fact, he said, "I am the way, the truth and the life."

Now I reach back into history to show the power and the love of our King. The year was 312. The Roman Empire was in power, and the pagan Constantine the Great was at war with an enemy. He himself was the enemy of Christians, whom he persecuted. In that year 312, he had a vision. A cross hung over the sun at noon with the words, "In this sign conquer." That night, Christ our King appeared to him. He told Constantine to paint the cross on his soldiers' shields. He won the battle that followed. He also ceased his battle against Christians, allowing freedom of religion. Thereafter, the Christian faith spread through the empire (See CONSTANTINE I in *New Catholic Encyclopedia*, vol. 4).

In the year 1899, Pope Leo XIII recalled that historic event and said the cross gave the Emperor the victory. Then the Pope added that now "another blessed and heavenly token is offered to our sight—the most Sacred Heart of Jesus, with a cross rising from it and shining forth with dazzling splendor amidst flames of love. In that Sacred Heart all our hopes should be placed...." The Pope called the world's churches to consecrate the human race to the Sacred Heart of Christ our King, and it was done. Years later, Pope Pius XI established this Sunday as the Feast of Christ the King each year. And so today, we honor our King and honor his Sacred Heart as well.

To what was Pope Leo referring when he spoke of another "heavenly token" given us, the Sacred Heart with a cross rising from it? What he was describing fits the visions of St. Margaret Mary which have been accepted as authentic by the Church. They began in 1673. Jesus appeared to her, showed her his Heart aflame with a cross surmounting it, and asked that the Feast of his Sacred Heart be celebrated yearly around the world. In addition to asking for devotion to that physical Heart which he took to love us with a human love, he asked for reparation to his Heart neglected and offended by our sins. He also asked for public worship of his Heart by the monthly Holy Hour, and First Friday Communions of Reparation.

Reparation is a key to undoing sins past. To make reparation is to repair for our sins. We heal the Heart we wounded by repenting, confessing our sins, and offering our prayers and works to heal the sinful world he came to restore and redeem. The *Catechism of the Catholic Church* says that the sacrament of Penance requires us to repent, confess, and "make reparation and do works of reparation" (#1491). By reparation we join Jesus in repairing and doing penance for the sinful and wounded world.

It would, then, be a bad error to picture Jesus as an offended lover moping about pining for love unreturned. Offended he is, but he is always concerned for *us* as well. He is grieved because many are rejecting his call to their own salvation. St. Margaret Mary saw that. She said, "It seems to me that our Lord's earnest desire to have his Sacred Heart honored in a special way is directed toward renewing the effects of redemption in our souls" (See the *Divine Office*, Feast of St. Margaret Mary, Oct. 16).

The *amende honorable*, the honorable amendment or reparation Jesus asked through St. Margaret Mary, was a concept well known in France. French law at times demanded an *amende honorable* in the form of a public confession of crime by one who had insulted royalty. The offended royal person sometimes accepted this public reparation, and asked no further punishment of the wrongdoer.

Jesus asks that we make this public reparation not only for ourselves but for other sinners too, to give him a kind of cause or "excuse" to forgive and save sinners he died for who are not responding. It's a touching request on his part, a kind of last-ditch effort to save the hardhearted, as he told St. Margaret Mary.

What, then, is required of us by our King? He taught us we are to love everyone on earth. Realistic love is a helping love. How help six billion people? By *prayer* for all, and service to some.

Now I come to that help which I said I would propose to keep us faithful servants of our good King and Lord.

That help is the Apostleship of Prayer, the League of the Heart of Jesus. It keeps us faithful in both prayer and service. In prayer it unites us with the Vicar of Christ for the critical needs of the Church and the world. In the way of service, it helps keep us disposed to do and endure whatever the Lord wants of us daily, as is required of every faithful follower. "Taking up one's cross each day and following Jesus is the surest way of penance" (CCC #1435).

Now back into history once again, to describe the origin, power and meaning of the Apostleship of Prayer—the A.P. for short—and invite you to join today.

First the origin of the A.P. The year was December 3, 1844, the Feast of St. Francis Xavier, the great missionary. The saintly Fr. Francis X. Gautrelet was in charge of the spiritual needs of seminarians. He saw they were restless in their studies, eager to go off to the missions. "Be apostles now," he told them, "apostles of prayer. Offer all you are doing every day in union with the Heart of our Lord for what he wishes, the spread of the kingdom for the salvation of souls." They took him up, and the Apostleship of Prayer was born.

It was later given the subtitle, "The League of the Sacred Heart," by his successor, Fr. Henry Ramiere. Fr. Ramiere found his vision of the A.P. expressed in those words of St. Paul to Timothy: "I ask that supplications, prayers, petitions and thanksgivings be offered for everyone (for).... This is good and pleasing to God our Savior, who wills everyone to be saved and to come to knowledge of the truth" (1 Tm 2:1-4).

Ramiere saw how prayer makes our love for the whole human race meaningful. It makes use of the power of the Almighty. He said God put the air we need as near as our mouth—and put prayer just as near. Prayer in union with the Heart of Jesus is invincible.

The founders of the A.P. call members to say the Morning or Daily Offering each day. You'll find that prayer on the cards in the pews. Please take one and pass the rest to your neighbors; then kneel and say the prayer with me, and I'll explain its meaning and power.

"O Jesus...."

Did you notice that in the Daily Offering we join with Jesus in *more than prayer?* We share his yoke by offering everything we think, feel, say and do in union with his Holy Sacrifice.

Pope Pius XII said the A.P. "is not merely one of prayer. By its very nature it holds out to its members the perfect Christian life and enables them to live it.... No one worthy of the name of Christian can sanctify himself and yet ignore the eternal salvation of others, forgetting 'that the Lord gave to everyone a commandment concerning his neighbor.'" The Pope added, "We call the League a perfect devotion to the Sacred Heart of Jesus, so perfect that the two cannot be separated" (9/19/1948, Letter of Pius XII to J.B. Janssens, General of the Society of Jesus). Popes Pius XII, Paul VI and John Paul II urged members of all organizations to join the A.P. for its spiritual power. John Paul II said the A.P. is "right in line" with Vatican II "which presents the Eucharistic Sacrifice as the foundation, center and culmination of all Christian life" (Address of 4/13/85 to the A.P.).

Why is the A.P. so helpful?

Because it joins each of us personally in a friend-to-friend way with the Heart of Jesus. Pope Leo XIII, still praised for his great labor encyclical, called his encyclical on consecration to the Heart of Christ our King "the greatest act of my pontificate." Why? Because the labor encyclical called to reform, but love of our King motivates and empowers reform. Consecration to the Heart of our King did in fact inspire people to develop "the social reign of the Sacred Heart in the reform of harsh conditions in the working place" (See F.J. Powers, S.J., *Spirituality of the Heart of Jesus*, pp. 32-33).

The A.P. helps us live "the perfect Christian life" by uniting with Jesus in prayer, work and word, thus making use of the share we received at baptism in Christ's priestly, kingly and prophetic powers. As you saw in the Daily Offering, we pray with the Pope for his special intentions for the Church and world which he gives us each month. We make our offering through the Immaculate Heart of Christ's Mother, his most loving, faithful, loyal, zealous comrade, disciple and enemy of sin and Satan the world has ever known. She is our Mother too, in the life of grace.

Now I invite you to join or renew membership in the Apostleship of Prayer, the League of the Heart of Jesus, as a way of saying to your King today, "I am at your service of love," and to make your life so meaningful nothing will be wasted. There are no dues, meetings, signatures, or obligations under sin. You simply agree to say and live the Daily Offering, and to say at least a decade of our Lady's rosary daily. I'll read the pledge so you'll know what you're pledging, then invite you to stand and repeat it.

> LORD JESUS CHRIST—
> I WISH TO BE A MEMBER—
> OF THE APOSTLESHIP OF PRAYER—
> THE LEAGUE OF THE HEART OF JESUS.—
> I PROMISE TO SAY—
> AND WITH YOUR HELP TO LIVE—
> THE DAILY OFFERING.

To join the A.P., stand now and repeat after me....

I NOW ADMIT YOU AS LIFELONG MEMBERS OF THE APOSTLESHIP OF PRAYER, THE LEAGUE OF THE HEART OF JESUS.

HOMILY OUTLINE:

* "My kingdom does not belong to this world." The unique King, with unique king-followers like St. Louis IX.

I. To Appreciate Our King: A Reflection on Leaders
* Plato's idea of love of truth vs. Christ, who is the Truth.
* Story of Constantine: Vision and victory; restoration of Christian rights and spread of the faith.
* Pope Leo: new sign of victory: Heart of Jesus, cross and flames of love; consecration of all to Heart of Christ the King.
* Pope's description fits the visions of St. Margaret Mary in 1673 etc.; what Jesus called for.
* Reparation's meaning and purpose; like the *amende honorable*.
* What, then, does our King require? Love all: by prayer/action.

II. A Special Help to be Faithful to Our King: A.P., League
* Back to history for its origin in 1844: Fr. Gautrelet's story.
* Based on St. Paul's instruction to Timothy.
* The A.P.'s power: prayer in union with Heart of Jesus.
* The Daily Offering. TAKE UP CARD....
* The A.P is more than prayer: promise to do God's will daily.

III. Why is the A.P. So Helpful?
* Because it joins us to Jesus as friends of his Heart;
* It inspires us to do what he wants, as Leo XIII saw;
* It makes us prayer partners of the Popes, who give us their monthly intentions;
* It joins us to Jesus in more than prayer: we share yoke, give all in union with Holy Sacrifice.
* Pius XII: "perfect Christian life."
* All in and through Immaculate Heart....

IV. Invitation to join — and why:
* Makes life meaningful; no dues, meetings, signatures or obligation under sin;
* Just say and try to live the Daily Offering as expressed in the following pledge:
  LORD JESUS CHRIST—
  I WISH TO BE A MEMBER—
  OF THE APOSTLESHIP OF PRAYER—

THE LEAGUE OF THE HEART OF JESUS.—
I PROMISE TO MAKE—
AND WITH YOUR HELP TO LIVE—
THE DAILY OFFERING.
I NOW ADMIT YOU AS LIFETIME MEMBERS OF THE APOS-
TLESHIP OF PRAYER, THE LEAGUE OF THE HEART OF JESUS.

"C" — Solemnity of Christ the King   2 Sam 5:1-3
Col 1:12-20
Lk 23:35-43

SPIRITUAL FOUNDATION STONE: THE APOSTLE OF PRAYER'S DAILY EXAMEN

HOMILETIC REALIZATIONS

In Vatican II's *Decree on the Life and Ministry of Priests*, we priests are told of the necessity of teaching our people to grow in prayer and to learn to listen to the Spirit—that is, to discern spirits (##5-6). Though we may not often put it that way, the daily examination of conscience, when well done, is truly a practice of prayer and discernment of spirits, and one of the most crucial of such practices.

Consequently, the homily that follows is one of the most practical helps to spiritual growth that parishioners could ask for. They are likely to recognize it as such, too, as their response to the author's preaching of this homily has taught him. Many proved eager to take the offered handout (see below) that outlines the practice of the Evening Examen.

The homily given here flows from three fonts: the Gospel of the Solemnity, the spirituality of the Apostleship of Prayer, and the *Spiritual Exercises of Saint Ignatius*. The *Spiritual Exercises*, together with devotion to the Heart of Jesus, are the primary sources of Apostleship of Prayer spirituality.

We all need *methods* to grow spiritually, as the homily affirms with the help of forceful examples. One writer said wisely, "Augustine's *Confessions* are written as if in answer to the plea, 'Teach us to transcend!' He knew from experience that motive and goal mean little without a practical plan of action." St. Ignatius's way of the Examen is a simple but profound prayer method.

The joining of Daily Offering and Evening Examen provides

people with a mature spirituality, centered on the Heart of Jesus, that generates *true* devotion, the loving eagerness to do God's will in all the thoughts, words and actions of life. This homily helps to that purpose. If some of the hearers who are not making the Daily Examen adopt the practice for life, the homily will surely please the King on his Feast Day.

The Feast of Christ the King was originated by Pope Leo XIII to consecrate all of humanity to the Heart of our King. May we continue the work with the heartfelt dedication it deserves.

SUGGESTED PENITENTIAL RITE

To prepare ourselves to offer the Holy Sacrifice of Christ our King on his Feast Day, let us call to mind our sins. Do we daily examine our conscience to uncover our failures in the service of our King, and to amend our lives? Are we dedicating our lives to the coming of his kingdom, and our hope of sharing it forever? (Pause, then continue with the formula: Lord Jesus, you are mighty God…).

SPIRITUAL FOUNDATION STONE:
THE APOSTLE OF PRAYER'S DAILY EXAMEN

"We are only paying the price for what we have done, but this man has done nothing wrong."

Allow me to lighten for a moment the solemn mood induced in us by our Savior on the cross. I do it to contrast the profound examination of conscience which the good thief made with a less penetrating one by a little boy. The boy went to his teacher and said, "Miss Jones, I don't mean to scare you, but when my daddy saw my report card he said, 'If the next one is like this, somebody is going to get a licking!'"

Isn't it true that the other malefactor on the cross made even a poorer examen of conscience than that little boy? All he could think of was to imagine that others were failing him, not that he was failing!

Today I want to invite you to join the Apostleship of Prayer, the League of the Heart of Jesus, as a service to Christ in the spirit of the man we have come to call **Dismas the Good Thief.**

In the very hour our Savior-King died in torment, scorned as a false Messiah, Dismas served and honored him with a marvelous examination of conscience and a mighty act of faith. We in our turn are helped to serve and honor our King by the Morning Offering, and the evening Examen of Conscience. By the Morning or Daily Offering, as it is also called, we daily consecrate everything to the service of Christ. By the evening Examen of Conscience, we stay on course.

In response to Dismas, Jesus said, "I assure you, this day you will be with me in paradise." Any "day" in paradise is the Eternal Day, the Day we all hope to be called to by our Savior-King on the final day. We have a lot to learn from Dismas to help us win that grace. Let's observe more closely how he achieved that all-but-impossible act of recognizing the Savior of the world in the naked, disgraced, condemned man beside him.

Dismas' own words about Jesus give us the clue: "This man has done nothing wrong.... We deserve it, after all. We are only paying the price for what we've done." Clearly, Dismas had made an earnest examination of conscience and consciousness: weighing not only his own conduct, but that of those around him. Jesus' behavior won his heart; his fellow-criminal's conduct only wounded it further. The movement of his heart brought on by Jesus helped Dismas admit his guilt at last. We need to examine our consciences as honestly.

Before I describe the Daily Examen of Conscience, please say with me the Daily Offering, as Dismas made his prayer to Jesus. Pick up the Prayer Cards in the pews, pass them to one another, and pray with me. Joining the Apostleship of Prayer means pledging to say and live the Daily Offering, plus a decade of Our Lady's rosary. There are no dues, meetings, or obligations under sin. Please kneel and join me now:

O Jesus, through the Immaculate Heart of Mary...

Now please pocket your card and be seated, as I explain how

we can make that Daily Offering more powerful by joining it to its spiritual partner, the Daily Examen.

Catholic wisdom teaches the necessity of the daily examen.

It helps us check on how we're living the Morning Offering, and make needed corrections tomorrow. What good does it do to offer our King every prayer, work, joy and suffering of the day if we don't live out our promise? Let's not be like the son in one of Jesus's parables who said *yes* to his father's request, but never did what he asked. We even want to do better than the other son, who said *no* to his father, but obeyed in the end.

How important is the Examen? The *Wall Street Journal* reported that the most frequent cause of business failures is lack of good record keeping. Jesus taught the same lesson about the failure to gain eternal life, in the story of the wealthy farmer. He gloated over his full barns, not knowing he would die that very day and have to give God an account of his miserliness. His money matters were going well, but his business of life was an utter disaster. He was unaware of it because he was no examiner of conscience.

It's hard to recognize and admit our sins. It takes daily effort. We need to uncover not only the wrong we do but the good we fail to do. Each evening we need to examine the moods and impulses we had that day. Did we act on the inspirations and good impulses that came from our hearts, from good people around us, from the angels, and from God himself? Asking and finding the answer to that question is what we call *the consciousness examen*. Are we doing the work of Jesus who said, "Take my yoke upon you"? It is what the Apostleship of Prayer urges us to do.

Don't go to bed without a Daily Examen of Conscience. It's better than a sleeping pill. I'll describe the Examen St. Ignatius gave us. He says, "The purpose of this Examination of Conscience is to purify the soul and aid us to improve our confessions." The *Catechism of the Catholic Church* teaches the need of the Daily Examen for continuing conversion, and as the proper preparation for Holy Communion (##1435, 1454).

St. Ignatius's prayerful daily examen consists of five points: we give thanks; we pray for light; we make our examen; we ask forgiveness; we resolve to amend with God's grace.

First, **we give thanks.** This beginning reflects the genius of Catholic life. We don't start with our discouraging self; we begin with God: "My praise and thanks, Lord! You care for me even when I sin. Help me be sorry now as I examine myself and try to grow more like Jesus. Amen."

This approach is immensely important! Judas looked at himself and despaired. Dismas looked at Jesus and hoped. With eyes on Jesus crucified for love of us we'll never despair.

Second, **we pray for light:** Jesus, lend me your eyes. Lend me your Heart. Make my heart pulse with yours, so I'll see and feel my sins and failings, and rid myself of them.

Third, **we demand an account of our conscience.** We review our thoughts, words, and deeds, over the hours and the people we've been with. We review our duties and relationships in family, friendships and workplace.

I already mentioned a key part of this review: the examen of consciousness. God really does guide us. We need to examine whether we're responding to the Holy Spirit as he draws us to noble deeds in Jesus' likeness. Try to re-envision moments of the day when you felt inspired to something more, something better. Try to sense again any feeling or drawing to action to which you didn't respond. If you find one, examine it and ask, "Lord, was this a call from you? Am I growing closer to your Heart, or am I saying secretly, 'I don't want to give more'?" So we check not only on our sins but on our response to the call to saintliness.

Our Daily Examen needn't take a lot of time if we can't spare much. As G.K. Chesterton said, a thing worth doing is worth doing half well. But when we have the time we should go deeper: go over the Ten Commandments, the Seven Capital Sins, and the five senses, and see how we're doing. An appealing practice is to compare the way we use our five senses with the way Jesus, Mary and Joseph used theirs.

In the fourth point, **we ask pardon.** We think of self as the prodigal son or daughter returning to our Father. We use a memorized act of contrition, or one from our own heart. We tell Jesus how sorry we are that we weren't more faithful, true, loyal companions at his side doing the work of salvation. Or we rejoice that we were.

If we've sinned mortally, we make an act of perfect contrition. We tell God we dread losing heaven and fear hell, but are even more sorry for offending him. It wins us forgiveness at once. If we died before getting to confession we'd be saved.

Fifthly and finally, **we resolve to amend our lives.** We glance at the coming day. Do I have to show a family member or some co-worker a special kindness? Is there a situation to avoid, a moment in the day in which I could slip in a prayer, a sick person to visit, a friend to phone? One resolution is enough. Many are useless.

Close with an "Our Father."

I conclude by inviting you to join the A.P., or to renew your membership. I'll first say the pledge, then invite you to repeat it after me:

LORD JESUS CHRIST—
I WISH TO BE A MEMBER—
OF THE APOSTLESHIP OF PRAYER—
THE LEAGUE OF THE HEART OF JESUS.—
I PROMISE TO SAY—
AND WITH YOUR HELP TO LIVE—
THE DAILY OFFERING.
Now repeat after me....
NOW I ADMIT YOU AS LIFELONG MEMBERS OF THE APOSTLESHIP OF PRAYER, THE LEAGUE OF THE HEART OF JESUS.

HOMILY OUTLINE:

* "We are only paying the price for what we have done...."
* The little boy's examen of conscience—and the malefactor's.
* TODAY: invitation to join A.P. as service in spirit of Dismas.
* Dismas' marvelous examen and mighty act of faith.

* We follow suit with Daily Offering and Evening Examen.
* Jesus answered Dismas' plea with Eternal Day—and will ours.
* How did Dismas ever do it? His words are the clue: comparing Jesus with self: An Examen of conscience/consciousness.
* Then a confession of guilt! So we must do.
* As Dismas prayed, please pray Daily Offering with me now.

I. **Catholic wisdom teaches the necessity of a Daily Examen:**
* It's partner and check on Morning Offering, and in-course correction.
* How important? Cf. *Wall Street Journal* and parable of farmer.
* *Sin?* Hard to recognize/admit our own, especially omissions.
* Examine moods, inspirations, impulses = Consciousness Examen.
* Are we doing work of Jesus who said "Take my yoke upon you"?
* I'll describe St. Ignatius' *method* and its purpose.

II. **A prayerful Daily Examen consists of five points:**
   1. *Give Thanks*: Genius of Catholic life: start with God, not self.
* Compare Judas with Dismas, imitate Dismas, and never despair.
   2. *Pray for Light*: "Jesus, lend me your eyes... heart... feelings."
   3. *Demand an Account of Our Conscience*: thoughts, words, deeds; then review response to Holy Spirit's drawings to noble deeds.
* When there is time: Go over 10 commandments, 7 capital sins, 5 senses.
   4. *Ask Pardon*: Act of Contrition... or Perfect Contrition.
   5. *Resolve to Amend*: Coming day. What needs doing/avoiding?
   6. Close with an "Our Father."

III. **In conclusion, I invite you to join the A.P.:**
   LORD JESUS CHRIST—
   I WISH TO BE A MEMBER—
   OF THE APOSTLESHIP OF PRAYER—
   THE LEAGUE OF THE HEART OF JESUS.—
   I PROMISE TO SAY—
   AND WITH YOUR HELP TO LIVE—
   THE DAILY OFFERING.
HANDOUT: **THE APOSTLE OF PRAYER'S DAILY EXAMEN**

First, **give thanks.** Reflects Catholic genius: like Dismas, not Judas; look on Jesus crucified, not on discouraging self.

Second, **pray for light:** Jesus, lend me your eyes, heart, to see my failings as you see them; help me to repent, and rid myself of them.

Third, **demand an account of conscience.** Go over thoughts, words, and deeds of day, over hours, people, places. Review duties, relationships, especially in family and workplace. Review not just conscience but consciousness: did I respond to Holy Spirit drawing me to Christ-like noble deeds through inspirations/impulses from my heart, good companions, angels, God? Am I growing closer to your Heart, Jesus, or saying secretly, "I don't want to give more"? Check not only on sin but on saintliness.

Needn't take long. But when time's available, go deeper. Go over the Ten Commandments, Seven Capital Sins, and use of the five senses. Compare the way I use them with the way Jesus, or Mary, or Joseph used his/hers.

Fourth, **ask pardon.** Return to Father of Love; express sorrow for not being more faithful, true, loyal, zealous companion living the Daily Offering, doing work of salvation at Christ's side. Make act of contrition.

Fifth, **resolve to amend.** Is there a need to show special kindness to someone, a situation to avoid, a pause each day where a prayer can be slipped in? Close with an "Our Father."

Chapter Four

Homilies of
ENROLLMENT IN THE
APOSTLESHIP OF PRAYER

THE LEAGUE OF THE HEART OF JESUS

Votive Mass of the Sacred Heart   1 Jn 2:2:29-3:1a
        Ps 23
        Mk 10:13-16

YOUNG MISSIONARIES OF THE HEART OF JESUS

HOMILETIC REALIZATIONS

Since children are the future of the Apostleship of Prayer, they are of crucial importance to its continuance. But the Apostleship of Prayer is also of immense value to them, as over a century of experience has shown, and many priests can witness. Its very nature draws them to Jesus heart-to-heart, inspires them to be his friends, companions, and faithful yoke-sharers in the work of redemption. Pope John Paul II called it a *must* that special attention be given to children in this work (*L'Osservatore Romano*, April 29, 1985, p. 5). So it is of prime importance to explain its nature to children, show how appealing it really is, and invite them to join.

The priest who reported the story of the little girl and the Three Golden Pennies which is recounted in the homily that follows is Fr. Mateo Crawley-Boevey, founder of the Enthronement of the Sacred Heart of Jesus.

As the author knows by experience, a fine way to end this homily is to have a supply of Sacred Heart Badges on hand at the altar (see p. 200 for source of supplies), and to invite any of the children who wish one to come up for it. The author has found the eager response heartwarming.

YOUNG MISSIONARIES OF THE HEART OF JESUS

"Amen, I say to you, whoever does not accept the kingdom of God like a child will not enter it."

I hope you children are happy to hear how much Jesus loves you. Did you notice that some of Jesus' followers thought Jesus ought not waste his time on children? They tried to brush the children away, but Jesus gave them a good, strong correction. It's as if he said: "Why should I be too busy for the children? They're just as important as anyone else!"

But someone might say, "Well, sure, we all love the children, and that makes them important to us, but everybody knows children can't **do** anything important."

I. Do you believe that? Do you think Jesus believes that? What are some important things even little children can do?

(In dialogue, try to draw from the children their way of describing the following things they can do: Love! — the best thing anybody can do. Love God, especially in Holy Communion. Pray. Do whatever God wants, like obeying parents and teachers. Be good, honest, kind, generous: all the virtues! Do whatever pleases God because at any age it helps us and helps others to be all God wants us to be, and helps us to be worthy to live with God now and forever).

II. You can be like certain young men who learned how to be missionaries right now. Here's their story:

They were studying to be priests, but they were tempted to sit around daydreaming of going to the missions like the great missionary St. Francis Xavier. You know how daydreaming keeps you from doing the studies you need to do now so you can really be prepared for what you will be expected to do in the future! The priest who cared for these young men knew it too, so he said to them: "Be apostles now, apostles of prayer! Offer everything you are doing every day in union with the Heart of our Lord for what he wishes, the spread of his Kingdom for the salvation of souls." And so they joined together and formed the Apostleship of Prayer, the League of the Heart of Jesus. Every day they said and lived the Daily Offering. That kept them faithful to prayer and faithful to doing their daily tasks.

In the pews you will find the Daily Offering Prayer Card. Please pick them up, hand them to your neighbors, and we'll say the prayer. Then I'll invite you to be missionaries by joining the Apostleship of Prayer. All you have to do is promise Jesus to be his special friend who will say this prayer every day and live it. And also you should say at least a decade of our Lady's rosary each day.

Please kneel and join me now in the prayer:
O JESUS THROUGH THE IMMACULATE HEART OF MARY....

Now put the card in your pocket and be seated again, and I'll explain a little more, then invite you to join.

III. Joining the Apostleship of Prayer can help you live more like Jesus the Boy Savior.

Every day he offered everything he did to God his Father for the salvation of everybody. As a boy he did the things every child does, but he did them without fail. He loved and obeyed his Mother and Father. He did what they told him. He helped around the house, and helped St. Joseph in the carpenter shop. He played with his friends, and he prayed a lot. You can do all those things too. If you offer them to Jesus in the Daily Offering, it makes you a missionary. You imitate Jesus, who was sent by the Father on the mission of winning salvation for the whole world.

Now I want to tell you about a young girl who was called by Jesus himself to do missionary work while still a child. We are told about her by a priest who knew her. She told him that Jesus talked to her when she went to Holy Communion. To see if it was true, he told her to ask Jesus for the conversion of a certain sinful man. When the little girl came back, she told the priest Jesus said that next time she came to confession, the sinful man would show up and go too.

She also told the priest that Jesus had asked her to be his missionary, but she said to Jesus, "I am too small." But Jesus made it clear she was not too small. He said, "You must earn golden pennies for this man's conversion." He explained that the first golden penny would be her prayers said from love; the second, her sacrifices, especially being obedient; the third, her promise never to miss Mass or Communion through her own fault, and always to go with love.

The girl had not even finished telling the priest her story when the sinful man walked in and asked the priest to help him make his first confession in many years. After that Fr. Mateo asked children everywhere to be missionaries of the Heart of Jesus by earning these golden pennies.

IV. Now I'm going to invite you to join the Apostleship of Prayer, the League of the Heart of Jesus as a special friend and missionary of the Heart of Jesus.

I will first say the promise by which you join, so you know beforehand what it pledges you to do. Then I'll repeat it and invite you to say it to Jesus with me.

LORD JESUS CHRIST—
I WISH TO BE A MEMBER—
OF THE APOSTLESHIP OF PRAYER—
THE LEAGUE OF THE HEART OF JESUS.—
I PROMISE TO SAY—
AND WITH YOUR HELP TO LIVE—
THE DAILY OFFERING.

I now enroll you or renew your enrollment in the Apostleship of Prayer, the League of the Heart of Jesus, the Kingdom of his love. If you say and live the Daily Offering every day you will be a close friend and true missionary of Jesus.

Votive Mass of the Sacred Heart

1 Jn 2:2:29-3:1a
Ps 23
Mk 10:13-16

SPECIAL FRIENDS
OF THE HEART OF JESUS

HOMILETIC REALIZATIONS

Is it not important, in working with children, to inspire them to become all that they can, and yet help them realize that the way to greatness is most often the little way? That is surely one of the lessons which St. Thérèse, Doctor of the Church, has taught so plainly. But the Apostleship of Prayer taught it to millions before she was born.

The very lifeblood of the Apostleship of Prayer is in doing our common garden variety of actions well and religiously, in accord with our state in life, that, normally, we most serve and please God. Vatican II's *Constitution on the Church in the Modern World* is rich with this teaching which is of the essence of the A.P. In reflecting on socioeconomic life it observes: "Indeed we hold that by offering his labor to God a man becomes associated with the redemptive work of Jesus Christ, who conferred an eminent dignity upon labor when at Nazareth he worked with his own hands" (#67).

The homily that follows attends to both aspects of the lesson children need. Aspire to heroic deeds for God, like St. Tarcisius, but take up the simple, practical means to serving him that the Apostleship of Prayer has proven to work so well that it has received endless praise and support from Rome.

When the Secretary of State sent the letter giving Pope Paul VI's high approval of the post-Vatican revision of the Statutes of the Apostleship of Prayer (March 27, 1968), he tendered the Pope's extraordinary praise as well. Citing the various ways that the revised

Statutes reflect the documents of Vatican II, and aware of the many millions of members of the Apostleship, he wrote that "All this increases the joyful hope of spiritual profit, which the Supreme Pontiff places in the almost numberless multitude of suppliants, who under the guidance of the Vicar of Christ and closely united with him, continue each day to offer to God their prayers, works and sufferings for the needs of the Church. It is with even greater solicitude that he commends this devoted association to all the children of the Church in whatsoever state of life they may be in. Other assistance of such strength and accessibility to all can scarcely be found...." (Reprinted in the 1968 Statutes, Apostleship of Prayer, Borgo Santo Spirito 5, Rome, Italy). In this passage, the "children of the Church" are both the young and the old; in the homily that follows, they are the young and tender little ones, about whom the Lord says, "Of such as these is the Kingdom of God." They will recognize and respond to the Apostleship if it is presented rightly, for in their unspoiled way they will see in their own simple way what the Pope sees.

SPECIAL FRIENDS OF THE HEART OF JESUS

"Let the children come to me; do not prevent them, for the kingdom of God belongs to such as these."

Did you notice that when some of Jesus's followers thought he was too busy for children, Jesus set them straight? He always has time for children. Jesus is telling us that he is a special friend of children. And he wants children to be special friends of his.

I'm going to say more about friendship, but first I want to give you an "Are You Awake" Test: What is the biggest room in the world? *(Invite a response from the children. The answer: The room for self-improvement!)*

I. **Now I want to say more about friendship, especially friend-ship with Jesus.**

There was a very bright teacher of English who didn't go to the dictionary to find out what the word "friend" means. He told his students that he learned what it meant from experience. "A friend," he said, "is the one you go to when you need help." He had learned that some people you go to for help will give you plenty of excuses, but a true friend will give you plenty of the help you need.

If you believe Jesus is your true friend, you will spend time with him, for friends love to be together. You can spend time with Jesus by prayer and visits to Jesus in the Blessed Sacrament. A very special way of spending time with him is by receiving him in Holy Communion, and telling him how much you love him, and feeling his great love for you.

Jesus also wants you to come to him when you need or want something. He wants you to ask him for it, but he also wants you to tell him that if he knows it's not good for you, please give you something better for you. He will be hurt if you don't ask. He will know that means you don't count much on him as a friend should, or care a lot for him, or trust him very much.

II. But there is another side of our friendship with Jesus that I have to talk about.

I'll do it by telling the story of a boy-Saint of ages ago. His name was Tarcisius. He lived in the third century when Romans persecuted Christians. He was entrusted to carry Holy Communion to some people in prison. We don't know why. Maybe it was because there was no one else available, or maybe because some priest thought the unfriendly unbelievers on the streets wouldn't bother a boy.

But they did. A mob gathered around him and asked what he was carrying. He wouldn't tell them, because the Blessed Sacrament was too holy to allow them to get hold of. So they kept beating him with sticks and stones until he fell down dead. Strangely, when they turned over his body, they could find no trace of the Holy Sacrament either in his hands or in his clothing. But the greater miracle is that a young boy was brave enough and loving enough to be a martyr for Jesus.

The other side of friendship that this true story brings out is this: Not only do we go to our friend Jesus for help, but he comes to us for help, as he did to Tarcisius. Does that surprise you? I hope not.

God could do everything by miracle, but he does many things in a much more loving way than by working miracles. He redeemed us by dying on the cross for us. He could have done it by a miracle but that was not loving enough to suit either our heavenly Father or him.

And so when he became a man by being born of the Virgin Mary, he, like other people, needed friends for love and for help. And he still does. In fact he said, "Take my yoke upon you and learn from me, for I am meek and humble of heart, and you will find rest for yourselves. For my yoke is easy and my burden light." I think most of you know that a yoke is the harness they put on two animals so that together they can pull a wagon or a plough that is too heavy for one. Jesus is telling us that it is the Father's plan that he should have help to do the work of bringing the kingdom of God, and we who love him have to give it.

There are almost as many ways of giving that help as there are people, but there are some things we all should do. We need to love God and our Blessed Mother and one another; to pray and go to Mass; to keep the commandments, and to help one another.

III. But today I want to talk about a simple, wonderful way to give our Lord everything we are and do by joining the Apostleship of Prayer, the League of the Heart of Jesus.

As members of the Apostleship, you simply say and try to live the Daily Offering.

In the pews you will find the Daily Offering Prayer Cards. Please pick them up, hand them to your neighbors, and we'll say the prayer. Then I'll invite you to be missionaries by joining the Apostleship of Prayer. All you have to do is promise Jesus to be his special friend and help him by saying this prayer every day and living it every day, and saying a decade of our Blessed Mother's rosary.

Please kneel and join me now in the prayer:

O Jesus through the Immaculate Heart of Mary....

Now put the card in your pocket and be seated again, and I'll explain a little more, then invite you to join.

If you say and live that prayer, you will give your whole life to Jesus, as he gives his life to you. As you and Jesus become closer and closer friends, you will want to go to Mass and Holy Communion whenever you can. You will try to use your five senses like Jesus and Mary, in good, healthy and holy ways, and never in sinful ways. Before sleep, you will spend a couple of minutes to consult with Jesus by a brief examination of conscience. If you find any sins or selfishness, you will tell Jesus you are sorry. Then you will be ready for a good, peaceful sleep in the arms of God your Father, to rest for another day.

All of this is summarized in four WATCHWORDS: Pray—Receive Communion—Sacrifice—Save Souls. Then you will be a special friend of the Heart of Jesus, his companion in work and play.

If you want to promise Jesus to live this way by saying and living the Daily Offering, and saying a decade of our Blessed Mother's rosary each day, you can join the Apostleship of Prayer right now. I will first say the promise by which you can join, so you know beforehand what it pledges you to do. Then I'll say it again and invite you to repeat it after me.

LORD JESUS CHRIST—
I WISH TO BE A MEMBER—
OF THE APOSTLESHIP OF PRAYER—
THE LEAGUE OF THE HEART OF JESUS.—
I PROMISE TO SAY—
AND WITH YOUR HELP TO LIVE—
THE DAILY OFFERING.
Please repeat after me....

I now enroll you or renew your enrollment in the Apostleship of Prayer, the League of the Heart of Jesus, the Kingdom of his love.

"ABC" — Feast of the Holy Family   Si 3:2-7, 12-14
                                                 Col 3:12-21
                                                 "A" — Mt 2:13-15, 19-23

FAMILY CONSECRATION
TO THE HEARTS OF JESUS AND MARY

HOMILETIC REALIZATIONS

What sane person would construct a building with crumbling bricks? Yet our society, built of families, fails to take the means to restore the health of disintegrating families. We in the Church must take the means, for the Church too is built of families and children of families.

The means to family health that the homily which follows provides is twofold: It invites those at Mass to enroll or renew membership in the Apostleship of Prayer; and it urges them to go home and consecrate their families to the Hearts of Jesus and Mary. The two steps are crucial. The personal enrollment is to a way of life that avoids inactive sentimentality: we must live our life of prayer and service, not just emote over it. Built on this foundation, the consecration of the home will bear far more fruit.

Who would deny that the Feast of the Holy Family is an ideal time to draw each family to consecrate itself to imitate the Holy Family? But if we think human means are adequate to restore society, we will take little interest in this devotional solution to deep family disorders. If, however, we believe that God alone can restore families to health and holiness, and society with them, we will not hesitate a moment to call families back to him in the simple ways the homily presents. They will set in motion the dynamic between individual families and the Holy Spirit that has all the power required to move hearts to make the needed changes.

St. Francis Xavier grew up in a home that housed a large, gory crucifix, recalling the words of Jesus, "When I am lifted up from the earth, I will draw everyone to myself." Xavier is portrayed in adulthood going through vast parts of the world bearing a crucifix as the sign of salvation. Would he have become that great missionary if he had not been daily reminded in his youth that Christ loved him and delivered himself for him? Can we not count on the image of the love of the Heart of Jesus having a similar deep effect on the families that keep it before their eyes?

The family Prayer of Consecration to the Hearts of Jesus and Mary which follows the talk may be reprinted in parish bulletins for use by families at home; or, if it would not make the homily too long, the priest could recite it at Mass with the parishioners, and they could repeat it again at home when the whole family can be together.

Attractive leaflets with the prayer (#413), as well as the large wall-size pictures mentioned in the homily (#412), may be ordered from the Apostleship of Prayer (see page 200).

FAMILY CONSECRATION
TO THE HEARTS OF JESUS AND MARY

"Rise, take the child and his mother, flee to Egypt...."

John the Baptizer was born in Ain Karim, not far from Bethlehem, where Jesus was born. We heard in today's Gospel how Herod sent soldiers to Bethlehem and neighboring places to slaughter the little boys. In Ain Karim, they display a hollow stone which is said to have saved the baby John's life by concealing him when the soldiers came.

Today's anti-child mentality is more subtle but equally killing, from abortion to child violence. Even worse than the assaults on their bodies are the evils in society which lead them into sin as they grow up, and kill the life of their souls.

A Russian Catholic who survived Soviet communism sets an example that targets what I wish to propose today. When Soviet Communism began collapsing in 1989, she was interviewed in the

Church of the Transfiguration in Lvov in the Ukraine. Years before, Stalin had forcibly joined the parish to the Russian Orthodox Church. In 1989, the Catholic parishioners of the Church reclaimed it for Catholicism. The only visible change was an icon of the Heart of Jesus. The woman standing before the likeness of Jesus said with tears in her eyes, "I spent 17 years in Siberia for my faith" (*New York Times*, 12/11/89, p. A4).

Here is a lesson for our homes. How better signal that they belong to Christ than by the image of his Heart in our living rooms? It belongs there. The Fathers of the Church called the Christian family a little domestic Church. We can't tabernacle the Eucharist at home, but we can enshrine Christ's image in the heart of our homes.

My special desire on this Feast of the Holy Family is to enroll you in the Apostleship of Prayer, the League of the Heart of Jesus, and then have you go home and consecrate your family to the Hearts of Jesus and Mary.

It would be hard to make too much of this consecration. The family is the center of much of our life in Christ. It is also the building block of both Church and nation.

In 1986, Queen Elizabeth told her people in her annual Christmas message that the world's problems won't be solved "until there is peace in our homes and love in our hearts" (*Buffalo News*, 12/26/91, p. 1). As the home goes, so goes the nation. The millions of disintegrating families pose such religious, moral, social and economic problems there seems to be no solution until we restore the family.

In 1991, Pope John Paul II asked us to pray that young families may build a better world (Apostleship of Prayer intentions, Dec., 1991). That is a call to do more beyond the family, but first it is a call to attend to the bettering of family.

We can restore the family by following the family model God revealed.

God says in Genesis that he created man and woman in his image and likeness. But we need to attend more to the fact that by calling couples to increase and multiply, he extended the image to a family image. We Christians, who have been given the revelation of

God as Three and One, God as Trinity, should better appreciate the likeness of the human family to God. St. Paul says, "I kneel before the Father, from whom every family in heaven and on earth takes its name."

The Second Vatican Council said that God sent his Son into the world "to tell them about the inner life of God" (*Dei Verbum*, #4). Jesus did this not just by word, but by his life. He made the Holy Family of Nazareth the perfect human likeness of God on earth. When Pope Paul VI visited Nazareth, he spoke from the heart about how we should meditate on the life of the Holy Family to make it the model of our own families (*Liturgy of the Hours*, I, Feast of Holy Family, second reading).

Jesus created the family of the Church, and the Second Vatican Council said that Jesus "implied a certain likeness between the union of the divine Persons, and in the union of God's sons in truth and charity" (*Gaudium et Spes* #24). If the Christian family is the Church in the home, the likeness to God is profound in a Christian family. They share both human and divine life together.

What is a better symbol of that union than the Heart of Jesus, who binds our families together by his love? The heart of Jesus also binds us to his Mother, Mary. On the cross, Jesus first gave us his Mother, and then his pierced Heart, as if to tell us that the two gifts are inseparable.

To stress the value of devotion to his pierced Heart, Jesus revealed its mysteries to St. Margaret Mary to be communicated to us all. To stress his will that we honor Mary's Immaculate Heart as well, he sent Mary to the children at Fatima.

Here at Mass I will give you a chance to consecrate your life to the Hearts of Jesus and Mary through the Apostleship of Prayer, the League of the Heart of Jesus. Then I will explain how you can go home and consecrate yourselves as family.

To join the Apostleship of Prayer you simply pledge to say and live the Daily Offering, plus a decade of Our Lady's rosary. Please pick up the Daily Offering prayer cards in the pews and distribute them to one another. Now kneel and pray with me:

"O Jesus, through...."
Please pocket your prayer card and be seated.

You see how by that Daily Offering we join everything to Jesus in prayer and service for the coming of the kingdom and the salvation of all people. That "everything" includes in a special way our family life, where our love is lived out so deeply.

You know how Jesus, in the Gospels, lived family life as a loving, obedient Son. You know how he spoke sternly against every sin that does harm to marriage and family union. You know how he always had time for the little children, no matter how busy he was. What a lesson for parents in that!

In the revelations to St. Margaret Mary, Jesus made special promises to families. The Saint reported Jesus saying that where an image of his Sacred Heart is honored, "He will restore broken families and protect those that are in any difficulty." She added that "The laity will find in this lovable devotion all the helps necessary for their state in life: peace in their families, consolation in their work, the blessing of heaven on all their undertakings, consolation in their afflictions" (*The Letters of St. Margaret Mary Alacoque*, Letters 131, 141). Is there anyone who doesn't need these blessings?

To join the Apostleship of Prayer, the League of the Heart of Jesus, you need only repeat the pledge after me.

There are no dues, signatures, meetings, or obligations under sin. Your only promise is to say and live the Daily Offering, and to say at least a decade of Our Lady's rosary each day. If you belong already, you may renew your membership. For joining, or once a year for renewing, there is a plenary indulgence.

I'll let you hear the pledge first, and then invite you to stand and repeat it. Here is the pledge:

LORD JESUS CHRIST—
I WISH TO BE A MEMBER—
OF THE APOSTLESHIP OF PRAYER—
THE LEAGUE OF THE HEART OF JESUS.—
I PROMISE TO MAKE—
AND WITH YOUR HELP TO LIVE—
THE DAILY OFFERING.

Now stand and repeat after me....

NOW I ADMIT YOU AS LIFELONG MEMBERS OF THE APOSTLESHIP OF PRAYER.

To consecrate your family to the Hearts of Jesus and Mary you will find in the vestibule wall size pictures plus a Prayer of Consecration to the Hearts of Jesus and Mary. They are made available at far less cost than if you ordered them directly from the National Office of the Apostleship of Prayer, so please take advantage of this special opportunity we are providing to help all enroll their families. [The Prayer is also reprinted in the bulletin, so take that home as well.]

PRAYER OF CONSECRATION
TO THE HEARTS OF JESUS AND MARY

Eternal Father, your divine Son became Man to save and restore us all. He *consecrated himself for us*, to assure our consecration in truth. Send your Holy Spirit to consecrate me and my family to his Sacred Heart.

Jesus our Lord, *King and Center of all hearts*, your Heart was the center of the Holy Family. Make it the center of my family, to make it holy too. I long to have my family united to you and to one another, living the truth in love.

Mindful of your promise to bless and heal families centered around your Heart, we pray for family lives of peace and unity in you. Help us live by your truth in the family of your Church. We long for hearts like yours, and families living in love, sharing your mission of bringing the Father's love to every human being.

Mary ever Virgin, Mother of Jesus, by the Eternal Father's gift you are our Queen and Mother. We consecrate ourselves to your Immaculate Heart, that is ever centered in Jesus' Heart. May your motherly heart, his childhood guide, lead us to the truth and love that are his very Heart.

St. Joseph, head of the Holy Family, instil in us your love of the divine Heart of Jesus, and the Immaculate Heart of Mary. Train

us in the family life lived in your Holy Family. Guide our way home
to the Holy Trinity, to share with your Holy Family the life of God
forever. Amen.
    Apostleship of Prayer
    With Ecclesiastical Approval

HOMILY OUTLINE:

    * "Rise, take the Child...."
    * Ain Karim, Bethlehem close by; the hollow stone....
    * Today's anti-child killing & violence.
    * Russian woman's faith; Icon of Heart of Jesus: example for us.
    * Identify home as Christ's with image of his Heart.
    * Home: domestic Church: can't keep Eucharist, but can Image.
 **I. My special desire on this Feast: enroll you in A.P./the
    League, then have you go home and consecrate your fam-
    ily....**
    * Important! Family: center of life, Church and nation.
    * Queen Elizabeth, in '86: no solution to world problems but by
      peace in homes and love in hearts.
    * John Paul II: pray young families build better world.
 **II. We can restore the family by following the family model
    God revealed.**
    * Genesis: God's image in humanity is found in family.
    * Christian faith in Trinity; St. Paul's dictum.
    * Jesus revealed God's inner life via the Holy Family.
    * Paul VI: meditate on Holy Family as our family model.
    * Divine Family, Holy Family, Church Family, Christian fam-
      ily.
    * Jesus unites our families by his love, Mother, pierced Heart.
    * His Heart revealed to St. Margaret Mary, his Mother's at Fa-
      tima.
 III. Here, consecrate self via A.P.; at home, consecrate family.
    * Pick up cards and say "Daily Offering" with me now....
    * That prayer offers everything—especially our family life....
    * Jesus' example, teaching on family, love of children....

* Jesus made special promises to families via St. Margaret Mary.
* What family doesn't need them?
  I INVITE YOU TO JOIN THE A.P./LEAGUE OF THE SACRED HEART
* No dues, meetings, signatures, obligation under sin.
* Just say and live daily offering.
  THE PLEDGE:
  LORD JESUS CHRIST—
  I WISH TO BE A MEMBER—
  OF THE APOSTLESHIP OF PRAYER—
  THE LEAGUE OF THE SACRED HEART.—
  I PROMISE TO SAY—
  AND WITH YOUR HELP TO LIVE—
  THE DAILY OFFERING.
  I ADMIT YOU AS LIFELONG MEMBERS OF THE APOSTLE-
SHIP OF PRAYER, THE LEAGUE OF THE HEART OF JESUS.

"A" — Fifth Sunday of Easter   Ac 6:1-7
                                                            1 P 2:4-9
                                                            Jn 14:1-12

THE LEAGUE THAT SHARES CHRIST'S YOKE

HOMILETIC REALIZATIONS

Preaching to young people is a privilege and a challenge. This homily was prepared to be given in a very large parish at a Sunday evening Mass that was heavily attended by youths, and it met the challenge.

The broader goal of preaching to the young is surely to help them gain a vision of what they can do with their lives, realize that with God they can achieve it, master their fears, and find motivation to make the needed commitment and undertake the effort to live it out.

St. Margaret Mary went through those stages. She was only about 26 when her mystical experiences began in 1673, and St. Claude de la Colombiere was only about 34 when he guided her. The young are called to great things, and God often uses the homilist's voice to give the call. Watering down the summons is beneath our dignity, an offense to them, and a wound to the Church and the world.

A parish that teaches its young to pray and to esteem the power of prayer is a bastion of strength in the Church, and all the more so if the prayer is made apostolic as it is through membership in the Apostleship of Prayer. The Popes are the ones who seem most to appreciate the power of the Apostleship of Prayer with its tens of millions of members. Can we doubt that their voices raised each day around the clock and the world more powerfully than the roar of the seas and joined in the same plea for the needs of the Church and the world will win the favor of our heavenly Father? Can we doubt that he will often make their hands and hearts the very means by which the grace petitioned enters the world? Isn't that the grace the young people need to become what grace and destiny summons them to be?

SUGGESTED PENITENTIAL RITE

To prepare ourselves to offer this Holy Sacrifice let us call to mind our sins. To modify a well-known question, Were you there when I crucified my Lord? Were we there when you crucified our Lord? For that is the case, since "Christ died for our sins in accordance with the scriptures" (1 Cor 15:3).

So let us call our sins to mind with true sorrow and atonement, and ask to be washed anew in those sacred streams from Christ's pierced side. (Continue with the formula: "Lord Jesus, you are mighty God....")

THE LEAGUE THAT SHARES CHRIST'S YOKE

"Do not let your hearts be troubled.... Amen, amen, I say to you, whoever believes in me will do the works that I do, and will do greater ones than these, because I am going to the Father."

These words of our risen Lord are jammed with good news, astonishing promises and a call to action, and I'll invite you to join an association that believes him and intends to change the world.

An example to which they apply will help. A deeply Christian man distressed by Christian friends going on hopelessly about the evil state of society broke in and demanded to know, "What are *you* doing about it?"

The words of Jesus which I just repeated are saying something similar, but saying it much better. It's as if Jesus is saying to Christians anywhere who feel overwhelmed and hopeless, "Don't be troubled about affairs. I have overcome the world. Now its your turn.

I'm going to work through you and make you accomplish more than I did."

Do you have any trouble believing that? Then remember that Jesus spoke to probably less than half a million people in his lifetime. The Pope speaks to hundreds of millions in a day, and has influence around the world. We are on Jesus's team and on his Vicar the Pope's team, spreading the Gospel by prayer and action for the transformation and salvation of the world. That is a simple description of the facts.

What if a vast association or league arose which showed the power and promise of attacking and solving today's worldwide problems? Would you join? If yes, do it today, for that league has arisen, has tens of millions of members, and I'm going to invite you to join.

But first an excursion of the imagination. Over 50 years ago, the novelist Hermann Hesse wrote a fascinating novel, *The Journey to the East*. It's about a cryptic, mystical League, shadowy, mysterious, worldwide, with secret purposes and promises. As the story of the League unfolds, various members grow unfaithful. Some repent, and seek to be reconciled; more flighty members find new interests and drift away; others allow the purpose of the League to grow vague, lose faith, drop out, and even become enemies of the League.

Where did Hesse get his intriguing idea? Hesse was a Christian and a deeply religious man, and the story seems to be a parable about the League we call the Church. But Hesse's ideas may also have been influenced by a League in actual existence, begun a century earlier, and having many millions of members by the time he wrote his novel. It is called the Apostleship of Prayer, the League of the Sacred Heart.

It's time to describe the origin and purpose of this League and invite you to join. The date of the League's founding was December 3, 1843, the feast of the great missionary, St. Francis Xavier, who had traveled East three centuries earlier to change the world.

The founder of the League was Fr. Francis Xavier Gautrelet, a Jesuit priest who saw that the Jesuit seminarians he guided needed an in-course correction. Their dreams of going to the missions like

Xavier were distracting them from the hard studies needed to make them good priests and missionaries one day.

"Be apostles now," Gautrelet cried, "Apostles of prayer! Offer everything you are doing every day in union with the Heart of our Lord for what he wishes, the spread of his Kingdom for the salvation of souls." The young men listened, and the League of the Heart of Jesus was born. It was born especially in the heart of one student, Fr. Henry Ramiere, who, after he was ordained, spread the League around the world. He also wrote a book about the League which envisioned millions of members devoted to the Heart of Christ who would convert countless numbers to Christ and put love to work changing and transforming the world through prayer and hands-on service in every field and career. He knew prayer was all-powerful. He knew it could be done. But believers have to do it.

The God-Man himself first gave that call to league up with him. "Take my yoke upon you and learn from me for I am meek and humble of heart." Note the twofold call to heart-to-heart friendship, and to share his mission, his "yoke." When we respond, no action is too small to be precious, and none too daunting to dare.

Jesus put the call in a way beyond words when he allowed his side to be pierced. Looking at that pierced side, and mindful of St. Paul calling Jesus "the last Adam," the Fathers of the Church saw the new Eve, the Church, being born of the water and blood flowing out. We are that Church, whom the Father gives to Christ to share his yoke.

Popes grew so enthusiastic they gave the League special intentions to pray for each month, and still do. Pope John Paul II called the League "a precious treasure from the Pope's heart and the heart of Christ."

The power of the League can be seen from a comparison. A pump to help failing hearts transmit blood has been built. Wonderful! But what will help hearts failing to transmit love? What but the God-man's Heart, and hearts that become like his? They can make love course through the whole body of the human race, as the League works to do.

What do you have to do as a League member? Each day, League members work with Jesus by saying and living the Daily Offering. You'll find cards in the pews with the Daily Offering. Please pass them to one another, and say the prayer with me now....
"O Jesus through the Immaculate Heart..."
That Daily Offering commits us to prayer and action that can change the world. We'll look at some of its elements. In that prayer we daily make use of our baptismal share in Christ's kingly, priestly, and prophetic mission.

First, the kingly mission. Christ, creation's King, will restore every star and every atom to the Father. But he won't force any free wills. He wins each of us by love or not at all. Every human being will choose to join the restoration of all things, or be left out forever. So we work and pray that lost hearts will find their way back.

Christians *must* do this work. "For each believer, as for the entire Church," Pope John Paul II wrote in his 1991 Encyclical, *On Missionary Activity*, "the missionary task must remain foremost, for it concerns the eternal destiny of humanity and corresponds to God's mysterious and merciful plan."

This is exactly what Fr. Gautrelet and Fr. Ramiere had in mind. They learned it from St. Paul, who said, "I desire first of all that supplications, prayers, intercessions and thanksgivings be offered for all people."

By the Daily Offering every thought, word, and deed becomes a missionary act. Members rule their little part of creation in accord with our King's purposes. They rule over sin by ruling it out of their lives. Guided by the Holy Spirit, they make home and work place centers of the new creation.

Members also exercise their baptismal share in the priesthood. By the Daily Offering they join everything with the sacrifice of the Mass, the renewal of Calvary. The deeds small or great they perform through the day appear with the body of Christ on the paten wherever the Mass is being offered around the world. They consecrate the world to God. A crucial aspect of this priestly action is to make honorable reparation for sin. Christ called for that through St. Margaret

Mary, as he calls for it in all the Gospel texts that demand repentance. Jesus also called for a monthly Holy Hour and First Friday Communions of reparation. They atone for sins against the love of his Heart in the sacrament of his love.

Reparation restores the dignity of both the offended Lord, and the offending sinner. Friendship is restored. Reparation is a profound religious reality. Basically, it means *to repair*. We repair or throw out broken things. The world is broken by sin. We in the League make intense efforts to repair God's broken world by our work and prayer-power in Jesus.

Pope John Paul II put it best: the essence of reparation is to learn from the Heart of Christ the true meaning of life, and on the ruins of hatred and violence to build the "civilization of love," the "kingdom of the Heart of Christ." Here is the campaign to renew everything within us and outside us.

We also share Christ's prophetic ministry in word and deed. The Magi were led to the Lord by the star of faith. Today that star of faith is the well-lived Christian life shining out in the darkness of the world to draw all to Christ.

All that remains is for me to summarize the vision of the League and invite you to join. The heart of our religion is the Incarnation; the heart of the Incarnation is the Heart of Jesus. We join our hearts to his for love of him, and our hands to his hands for the love and service of all. Members promise to say and live the Daily Offering, and to recite at least a decade of Our Lady's rosary daily. There are no dues, signatures, or obligations under sin, just a commitment of love and friendship.

He came to us through her immaculate womb; we offer all to him through her Immaculate Heart. She is his Mother and ours; she is his most loyal lover and yoke-bearer, apostle, friend, companion and most faithful disciple. We imitate her and seek her prayers and counsel.

The Church is his own creation; her teachings are his own. We live and breathe the Church. The Holy Father gives the League two special intentions to pray for each month. They focus on a critical need of the Church or the world, and a critical mission need. We include them in the Daily Offering.

How become a member? One can join the Apostleship of Prayer, the League of the Heart of Jesus, informally just by saying the Daily Offering. But I invite you to join the League formally. Joining or renewing membership gains you a plenary indulgence under the usual conditions.

I'll first recite the pledge, so you know what you're pledging, then invite you to repeat it:

LORD JESUS CHRIST—
I WISH TO BECOME A MEMBER—
OF THE APOSTLESHIP OF PRAYER—
THE LEAGUE OF THE HEART OF JESUS.—
I PROMISE TO SAY—
AND WITH YOUR HELP TO LIVE—
THE DAILY OFFERING.

Now if you wish to join please stand and repeat after me....

I NOW ADMIT YOU AS LIFELONG MEMBERS OF THE APOSTLESHIP OF PRAYER, THE LEAGUE OF THE HEART OF JESUS.

I will only add that special groups are encouraged to form a league within the League to join their careers, works and apostolates the more closely to the Heart of Jesus and their own purposes and those of the League.

May you share the love of the Heart of Jesus, meditate on the vision of the League, and live the mission of the yoke. Together, in the spirit of the Church, we carry on the renewal of creation in the course of the journey to the promised land. In that land no renewal is needed, for there all things are new in Christ.

HOMILY OUTLINE

"Do not let your hearts be troubled... whoever believes in me will do the works that I do, and will do greater ones than these, because I am going to the Father."

I. **This astonishing promise is a call to action, and I'll invite you to join an organization that believes and intends to change the world.**
  * A question to hopeless friends; and what Jesus is saying to them.
  * Example of Pope-and-us fulfilling Jesus's promise.
  * If there were a League to attack these problems, would you join? There is!
  * Hermann Hesse's *Journey to the East.*
  * Source of his idea? The Church.
  * And probably the League of the Sacred Heart.
II. **Time to tell of origin & purpose of the league and invite you to join.**
  * Apostleship of Prayer founded Dec. 3, 1843, Feast of St. Francis Xavier, great missionary.
  * Motive: "Become apostles now, apostles of prayer!"
  * Thus the Apostleship of Prayer, the League of the Sacred Heart was born.
  * Hope of Fr. Ramiere for world conversion/transformation.
  * League spread round world.
  * Seeds of League: Invitation of Jesus: Take my yoke....
  * Pierced side, Fathers of Church; Eve-Church is Christ's helper.
  * Enthusiastic Popes give prayer intention.
  * Power of Apostleship of Prayer: comparison with heart-assist pump, Heart of Jesus, love.
III. **What do you have to do as a League member?**
  * Say and live Daily Offering; take Cards and say with me....
  * Commits us to prayer/action to save/change the world.
  * Makes active our baptismal share in Christ's kingly, priestly, prophetic mission.
  * Christ's kingly mission: Restoring all to Father; our work too....
  * John Paul II on this; St. Paul said same: Daily Offering makes all we do a missionary act.
  * Serve, rule sin out, make our home and workplace a new creation.
  * Priestly Mission: join each thought, word, deed to Mass....
  * Reparation (St. Margaret Mary): monthly Holy Hour, Holy Communion of reparation.

* Reparation "repairs" mutual dignity/friendship, heals world; cf. John Paul II.
* Prophetic Ministry: we are the new "star" of faith.
* Summary and Invitation to Join Apostolate of Prayer/League
* Religion of Incarnation; Heart of Jesus; Mystical body; hands of Christ.
* He to us via womb of Mary, we to him via Immaculate Heart of Mary: she the faithful one....
* Church and her teachings and Holy Father: his creation.
* Joining the League: No dues, signature, obligation under sin.
    LORD JESUS CHRIST—
    I WISH TO BE A MEMBER—
    OF THE APOSTLESHIP OF PRAYER—
    THE LEAGUE OF THE HEART OF JESUS.—
    I PROMISE TO SAY—
    AND WITH YOUR HELP TO LIVE—
    THE DAILY OFFERING.
    I NOW ADMIT YOU AS LIFELONG MEMBERS....
* Special groups can form a league within League for their purposes and that of League.
* Live mission of yoke—and reach promised land of heaven.

"A" — Eleventh Sunday in Ordinary Time   Ex 19:2-6
                                                Rm 5:6-11
                                                Mt 9:36-10:8

CONSECRATING DAILY LIFE
TO THE HEART OF OUR REDEEMER

HOMILETIC REALIZATIONS

To deliver this homily with conviction and felt devotion we need to dwell on the following proposition: *Without personal devotion to Jesus there is no Christianity.* In our time one Successor of Peter after another has praised devotion to the Heart of the God-Man as a supreme way of nourishing this personal devotion to Jesus. They treat devotion to his Heart as not just one more devotion, but as the central one which can and should suffuse all other devotions and activities.

Popes have also singled out the Apostleship of Prayer, the League of the Heart of Jesus, as the preeminent means of spreading the devotion. It is a great loss if pastors, swamped by multiplying parish activities, neglect the Apostleship. It deprives the faithful of a great resource for knowing and practicing devotion to the Heart of Jesus.

The work of life is setting priorities. This homily was written to facilitate the proper priority in these matters. It has been composed for the Eleventh Sunday of "A" cycle to be used in the years when it falls close to the Solemnity of the Sacred Heart, to proclaim his Heart to the many who do not come out for the Mass of the Solemnity, and to invite them to join the Apostleship of Prayer as a way to be more faithful to his divine Heart in prayer and service and love of the Mass.

This homily can be adapted to other Sunday Masses of the year by replacing the first paragraph with an apposite introduction taken from the Gospel of the day. Following this homily are suggested replacement paragraphs for adapting it to certain Sundays of the year. Also, Appendix One has a "Procedure for Enrolling in the Apostleship of Prayer at Mass." It complements these Enrollment Homilies for Sundays.

SUGGESTED PENITENTIAL RITE

To prepare ourselves to offer this Holy Sacrifice let us call to mind our sins and ask to be washed anew in the sacred streams from the pierced side of our Redeemer. (Continue with the formula: "Lord Jesus, you are mighty God....")

CONSECRATING DAILY LIFE
TO THE HEART OF OUR REDEEMER

"At the sight of the crowds, his heart was moved with pity for them because they were troubled and abandoned, like sheep without a shepherd."

Do not these words of Jesus tell us well how his Heart goes out to those whose life has become meaningless, and who have no idea how to find their way to a meaningful life? Where are they to look for meaning?

When Dr. Michael De Bakey was doing his pioneering work on a mechanical heart, little children showed him they possessed an exquisite sense of where the meaning of life lies. They asked the heart doctor a question worthy of the three wise men. "Doctor," they said, "can you love with this heart?" They were concerned about love. Aren't we all? God is love. God made us for love. Life's meaning is found in love.

But things go wrong. Have you ever had those weary days when the daily tasks seem meaningless? And those seasons of the heart when life itself seems meaningless?

What goes wrong? What often goes wrong is that we neglect the serious issues of life and death, heaven or hell. We cram life with trivia and even with sin until our hearts become trampled gardens where there is no room for love to grow.

What is the solution? It is to find the Heart of God and do the works of love. So many speak of love and so few of the works of love. Ask any parent if there's love without work! God speaks of the works of love from the first pages of the Bible to the last. He instructed the first couple to unite in love, have children, and take command of creation to support family life.

Today I want to speak of the Heart of Jesus and the Apostleship of Prayer as they call us to find and live life's meaning.

Jesus, during his time on earth, called us to find our meaning by entering his Heart and sharing his work all our days. "Come to me," he said, "all you who labor and are burdened, and I will give you rest. Take my yoke upon you and learn from me, for I am meek and humble of heart; and you will find rest for yourselves. For my yoke is easy, and my burden light."

Let us attend well to that call to learn of him and his loving Heart. How? By sharing his yoke; by *working* with him. Haven't we all discovered how well we come to know another person when we work with him?

Our Lord is calling us to do the work of salvation with him. "We have become partners of Christ" says the Letter to the Hebrews.

Our Lord didn't leave his invitation in mere words. He let his side be pierced and his Heart opened, as if to say, "There, the path is clear now. Enter my Heart through prayer, shared work, and above all, Holy Communion. Experience my love and return it."

The Fathers of the Church, meditating on Jesus's pierced side, saw its meaning. They saw the "last Adam," as Paul calls Jesus, and in the water and the blood coming from his open side they saw the new Eve, the Church, the bride of Christ, born of baptism and nourished on the Eucharist.

Despite these truths and mysteries, devotion to the Heart of

Jesus spread at such a snail's pace that some 300 years ago, like an impatient lover, Christ appeared to St. Margaret Mary repeatedly, revealed the love and mysteries of his Heart, and called her to spread the devotion, and the reparation owed him. He promised to send her his "faithful servant and perfect friend" to help her. And so Jesus sent her the Jesuit father, St. Claude de la Colombiere, and the two made Christ's desires known.

Zealous priests later founded the Apostleship of Prayer, the League of the Heart of Jesus, to spread the Devotion, and Pope after Pope has urged membership. What is the Apostleship of Prayer? It's a union of tens of millions of us from little kids up to the Holy Father who say and live the Daily Offering. We consecrate ourselves and everything we do and suffer and enjoy to Christ and with Christ for the salvation of all people.

Pick up the Prayer Cards at the ends of the pews. Pass them to one another, and say the prayer with me. Then I'll explain how the Apostleship works and invite you to join. There are no dues, no signatures, no meetings, and no obligation under sin—just devotion to Jesus. Now please kneel and say the prayer with me:

O, JESUS, through the... [After the prayer, invite them to pocket the card].

Did you notice that we return everything to the divine Heart of the God-Man through the Immaculate Heart of his Mother, because he came to us through her immaculate womb? What could please him more? We imitate her, the most loving, noble, sinless, zealous comrade, apostle, disciple and servant of Jesus. We draw close to her, for she is our Mother too. We say at least a decade of her rosary every day.

By that little prayer we daily find the meaning of life by joining in Christ's mission for the world's redemption.

This daily prayer helps us put to use the share in Christ's own kingship, priesthood, and prophetic ministry which we received at baptism and promised to use.

First, **His Kingship:** Sometimes we forget Christ is King not just in our churches. He is King of kings and Lord of lords, and he is reclaiming every atom of creation for God the Father. For those who join him, victory is assured, for he said at the Last Supper, "Fear not, I have overcome the world." Let's share his yoke and share his victory. When we wear the yoke of Christ there is never an empty day or empty action. Emptiness comes from building our own shabby little kingdoms.

Think of Christ himself. As a carpenter he worked for the salvation of the world just as he did on the cross. No matter what our station in life, no matter what we're doing, whatever our career, it's all useful and all to be consecrated to the bringing of the kingdom of God—whether we're sick in bed, or doing important work.

We are Christ's mystical body, completing his work. Where would the Church be without parents bringing new citizens of heaven and earth into the world? And rearing them in such a way there is hope they'll be good Christians and good citizens. All of this we consecrate. We consecrate our recreation as well as our labors, our joys as well as our sufferings. That's what Jesus did. He offered every action and experience of his to the Father for the redemption of the world. And in particular, through our share in Christ's kingly power, we rule over sin and rule it out of our lives. What is more kingly than that?

If we infuse Christ's values into our family life, personal relationships, work and politics and play, it all helps complete the redemption. Failure and suffering take on irreplaceable meaning. Christ's seeming failure and death was the sacrifice that redeemed the world. That is the mystery of our religion and of the Apostleship of Prayer.

Second, **His Priesthood:** Christ wasn't priest just on Calvary. He was priest at every moment, consecrating everything in creation. We share in that. Not everybody is an ordained priest. That's a special ministry. But we all share in Christ's priesthood by baptism. That's why all can offer the Mass with the priest, and why all can consecrate everything they do and put it on the paten with Christ at every Mass around the world. Think of parenting as a priestly act of life-giving and the kingly/queenly service of governing, and the prophetic ministry of forming the children in the faith.

Reparation is a special aspect of our priesthood. We offer reparation to the Heart of Jesus. He especially called for that through St.
Margaret Mary. What is reparation? It's *to repair*. When a thing
breaks we repair it or we throw it away. Sin broke God's world and
us with it. By acts of service, we help to build up the world. By penance we make reparation to the Heart of Jesus broken by our sins.
We heal his Heart by our love, our atonement, our prayers, our work
for the conversion of others. We stand with Christ repairing the
world.

Pope John Paul II said that "the true meaning of reparation
demanded by the Heart of the Savior" is to learn from the Heart of
Christ "the true and only meaning of life," and on the ruins of hatred and violence to build the "civilization of love," "the Kingdom
of the Heart of Christ."

Third, His Prophetic Ministry: To prophesy means basically
to speak God's message. Christ prophesied not only in word but in
deed. Christ hanging on the cross speaks louder than words: "I love
you, I die for you that you may find eternal life in me." Without his
message on the cross, would any of us be here today despite his
words? Like him, we have to give witness by our life and our words.

**Now I'll summarize what I have said and invite you to be
a member of the Apostleship of Prayer.**

The heart of our religion is the Incarnation—God become flesh.
The heart of the Incarnation, the Heart of the last Adam, is the human Heart he shared with us, the Heart to which the Heart of Mary
and the hearts of us all go out. In the Apostleship of Prayer we give a
central role to what his Heart loves most: his Mother, his Church,
his Vicar on earth.

We love the Church as Christ's creation and her teaching as his
own. We live and breathe the Church. It is the body of Christ where
we have eternal life. We love and honor the Holy Father, and pray
daily for his intentions and those of our bishops. The Holy Father
makes us his partners in prayer by giving us special intentions to pray
for each month.

I now invite you to join the Apostleship of Prayer. First, I'll say the pledge so you know what you're pledging, then ask you to stand and repeat it loud and clear.

LORD JESUS CHRIST—
I WISH TO BE A MEMBER—
OF THE APOSTLESHIP OF PRAYER—
THE LEAGUE OF THE HEART OF JESUS.—
I PROMISE TO MAKE—
AND WITH YOUR HELP TO LIVE—
THE DAILY OFFERING.

I NOW ADMIT YOU AS MEMBERS OF THE APOSTLESHIP OF PRAYER, THE LEAGUE OF THE HEART OF JESUS.

HOMILY OUTLINE:

Introduction: Meaningless and Meaningful Life
* "His heart was moved with pity for them because they were troubled and abandoned, like sheep without a shepherd."
* De Bakey and the wisdom of little children.
* God is love—made us for love; love = life's meaning.
* Things go wrong.... What...? Forget serious issues... trivia.
* The solution? Find Heart of God, do the works of love.
* So many speak of love, so few of its works.
* Ask any parent: Love without work? Cf. God to 1st parents.

I. Heart of Jesus and Apostleship of Prayer Help Us Find and Live Life's Meaning
* Jesus on earth called us to find life's meaning....
* Yoke! Of love and work of salvation with him.
* He didn't invite in mere words: Pierced Heart; cf. Fathers of the Church; Jesus to St. Margaret Mary because of snail's pace growth.
* Zealous priests founded Apostleship of Prayer and Popes urge us to join.
* What is the Apostleship of Prayer? A union of....
* Pick up Daily Offering Cards.... Say with me (No dues...).
* Did you notice? All through Mary: Model of love, obedience, and comradeship; we say her rosary.

* That prayer = daily life's meaning: join Christ's team for world redemption.

II. We Put to Use our Share in Christ's Kingship, Priesthood, Prophetic Ministry:

* We received these gifts at baptism and promised to use them.

A. Kingship:

* Not just in church: King of kings reclaiming creation.
* Christ the Carpenter: all he/we do brings Kingdom.
* We, his Mystical Body, Complete his work: Married couples; all of us. Emptiness goes when we unite all to Carpenter/Redeemer.

B: Priesthood:

* Christ wasn't priest just on Calvary....
* Not all are ordained priests, but all share priesthood by baptism; offer Mass with priest; consecrate all you do..., cf. parenting as priestly/kingly/prophetic work.
* Put on paten with him—prayers, works, joys, sufferings.
* Special priestly act: Reparation (John Paul II)

C: Prophetic Ministry:

* What it is; Christ is prophet more in deeds than words.
* We add our witness by lives like his.

III. Summary and Enrollment:

* Heart of our religion: Incarnation....
* We join self to Mary, Church, Pope and bishops.
* Church: His own creation, and her teaching....
* We love and obey Holy Father and bishops.... and pray for intentions.

IV. Enrollment: (Plenary Indulgence)

LORD JESUS CHRIST—
I WISH TO BE A MEMBER—
OF THE APOSTLESHIP OF PRAYER—
I WILL TRY TO MAKE—
AND WITH YOUR HELP TO LIVE—
THE DAILY OFFERING.

I NOW ADMIT YOU AS MEMBERS OF THE APOSTLESHIP OF PRAYER, THE LEAGUE OF THE HEART OF JESUS.

(The above homily can be adapted readily to the Sundays indicated below by replacing its first paragraph with the introduction provided under each Sunday listed.)

ADAPTATION TO "A" — 2nd Sunday of Advent

"Reform your lives. The reign of God is at hand...."

Today I ask you to respond to this Advent call to reform your lives and prepare the way of the Lord by consecrating or renewing your consecration to the Heart of our divine Redeemer through and with the Immaculate Heart of Mary, in the Apostleship of Prayer. Since reform is a call to the renewal of heart, let me begin with the heart.

ADAPTATION TO "A" — 1st Sunday of Lent

"Get away, Satan! It is written, 'The Lord your God shall you worship and him alone shall you serve.'" The Lord's example is nothing less than the Gospel in the flesh giving us strength to follow him in fidelity to today's reading. Christ condemns sin and summons us to redemption. Yet our culture condemns redemption by calling us to sin—as a right!

Our culture, good and wonderful in many ways, has lost its way in what counts most. It condemns as too demanding God's commands. It demands that we privatize natural law and religion and keep it out of the realm of law and justice. It denies that faith in God's revelation is as valid and even more valid a source of knowledge as information we obtain by faith in other persons by means of our whole educational system.

The Gospel puts the choice before us: follow God's law in freedom, or Satan's in slavery. So today I will invite you to a simple way of daily re-devoting your life to Christ and his way, thus giving true meaning to your lives. I will begin with a mechanical heart and end with the Heart that was pierced with love for us on the first Good Friday.

ADAPTATION TO "C" — 29th Sunday in Ordinary Time

"When the Son of Man comes will he find faith on earth?"

Today, Mission Sunday, we are concerned with the faith: keeping it, living it, and giving it. So I will speak about the Apostleship of Prayer, the League of the Heart of Jesus, because it is a great help to all three. And I will invite you to join the League, as Popes for a hundred years have been urging every Catholic to do. But let me begin with the heart.

"A" — Twelfth Sunday in Ordinary Time   Jr 20:10-13
                                                         Rm 5:12-15
                                                         Mt 10:26-33

THE APOSTLESHIP OF PRAYER
AND THE NEW EVANGELIZATION

HOMILETIC REALIZATIONS

God knows and the Church knows that if this old world is going to move forward into the age of the civilization of love, the Kingdom of the Heart of Christ, the Kingdom that will provide the climate for the conversion of all peoples, we need to get the troops active. That was the vision that originated the Apostleship of Prayer.
It is the vision brought to maturity by Vatican II and the Popes and
bishops since.

But getting the troops active requires the way of prayer and
service guided from within, and that way has often been thrust aside
in favor of more muscular and externally-directed ways and means.
In other words, the role of the Holy Spirit, and the need for the individual responding to the Holy Spirit, who is alone great enough to
guide this enterprise, have often been neglected. On the last day of
an August 7-11, 1996 Conference of Major Superiors of Men in Ar-
lington, Virginia, Franciscan Father Ken Himes, Moral Theologian
at the Washington Theological Union, pointed out that male religious were assuming leadership in social justice matters while the
laity "should have provided the obvious cadre of leadership."

Somehow or other, despite a century of intense Church teaching and documentation on social concerns and the faith-justice responsibilities of all believers, the laity, so many of whom are highly
educated and in positions of power and influence, have not adequately integrated their faith into their state in life, career, and daily
commitment to Christ.

The Apostleship of Prayer, based on the Gospels and the *Spiri-*

tual Exercises of St. Ignatius, is a powerful instrument for correcting this disorder. It recognizes that only the Holy Spirit can guide this world enterprise adequately, and inspire the roles and career calls which are needed and which need to be lived in the name of God. Of course, guidance from without, in encyclicals, books, preaching, and media, are needed but ineffectual without a more profound inner guide, the Holy Spirit himself. The Popes have stressed this for a century and more, and that is why they have so praised the Apostleship of Prayer as a marvelous instrument in the service of the coming of the Kingdom of God.

Keenly aware of such things, Pope John Paul II, speaking about the new evangelization, told religious that they must foster "an apostolic cooperation which respects and strengthens the responsibilities of each vocation in the Church." So must all priests.

The Curé of Ars said that "the priesthood is the love of the Heart of Jesus." Priests and Sisters knew that and spread the devotion and the Apostleship of Prayer far and wide, so that uncounted numbers of parishes and schools in the U.S. were centers, and the Church was enriched beyond measure.

In T.S. Eliot's pregnant lines, "We shall not cease from exploration / And the end of all our exploring / Will be to arrive where we started / And know the place for the first time." (*Four Quartets*, Little Gidding V). Isn't it time to return to the vision of devotion to the Heart of Jesus and the Association which spread it worldwide, the Apostleship of Prayer—and perhaps recognize its power and promise for the first time?

THE APOSTLESHIP OF PRAYER
AND THE NEW EVANGELIZATION

"Everyone who acknowledges me before others I will acknowledge before my heavenly Father."

Today we turn from Christ's saving deeds to our response. We have celebrated his Easter victory over sin and death and his Pentecost gift of the Holy Spirit. We have adored the Holy Trinity, celebrated the Feast of Christ's body and blood, and rejoiced in the Solemnity of his Sacred Heart.

Now the spotlight is on us, his people. Today's readings throw us into the fray. Jeremiah faces terror, false friends, and vengeance, and responds with a cry of trust in God our Champion. Paul depicts the whole history of sin, death, and the redemption in Christ that restores to us more than Adam lost. Jesus encourages us to fear nothing but the seductions that lead to the loss of eternal life. Give brave witness to him, and he will give saving witness about us to the Father in heaven.

We are hearing our Christian call in one of the hundred ways Jesus summons us to know him heart to Heart, and share his yoke and his work for the kingdom. In every Mass we pray to Our Heavenly Father for the coming of that kingdom, and we say to him, "Thy will be done on earth." There is only one will on earth that each of us can submit to the Father's will, and that is our own. Surely we welcome any help to do it.

It is in the name of and in honor of the Heart of our Savior that I offer you in the Apostleship of Prayer, the League of the Heart of Jesus, a great help to doing the Father's will as Jesus did it.

Membership in the Apostleship of Prayer commits us to say and live the Daily Offering. It follows up on the "Our Father" by taking the next step. In the Daily Offering we turn our lives over to our Lord Jesus day by day to do our part in bringing the kingdom. By the Daily Offering we pledge to Christ our will and our lives in accord with our state of life.

Before we look at that, a word to the young people present. If you've yet to chose a state of life, be sure to ask, *What is Jesus calling me to be and do?* Reflect and pray for light, and observe others to learn whether your call to holiness is to be lived in the single or married state, and whether the Lord may be inviting you to be a Sister or Brother or Priest. If you make the Daily Offering, and live it faithfully, the Holy Spirit will nudge you in the right direction each day, until you're able to make the right decision.

Now back to all of us. Whatever our state of life, we all need God's guidance day by day. If we make each day a gift to Jesus by the Daily Offering, he'll give us daily guidance. Nothing will be wasted. All will advance the eternal kingdom, which begins here on earth as the civilization of love, the kingdom of the Heart of Christ.

The Apostleship of Prayer was founded over 150 years ago to make us all missionaries in prayer and in action. The Statutes were revised many times to keep updated, to keep us in tune with the Church and the Popes. After Vatican II, they were revised to reflect its powerful message to every member of the Church that God is calling you to serve his Church.

Individually, all of us as members of the Apostleship, offer Jesus our prayer and our day for the needs of the Church and the world, according to the intentions in Jesus's own Heart, according to the intentions of the Holy Father and according to the opportunities our own lives provide. Then, as we live our day in keeping with our offering, we learn to do things in a more Christlike way.

A nightly Examen of Conscience leads to needed corrections, whether to stop something or to start something. It may lead to a simpler life style, the search for a more needed or meaningful career, or a new parish ministry. The manner the call of Jesus to change course in life comes to us may be more subtle than a phone call from a friend asking us to come and help, but it is just as real.

Popes have said that the Apostleship of Prayer is a perfect way to live the teaching of Vatican II. In its *Decree on the Apostolate of the Laity*, Vatican II tells you that your apostolate is as wide as the Church and the world. It says you are to be involved especially in "church communities, the family, youth, the social milieu, and national and international affairs" (#9). Anything good we do serves one of these purposes, or offers some other human service in the name of Christ.

Pope John Paul II supplements Vatican II by speaking of a "new evangelization." It is new in celebrating 2000 years of the grace of Christ and the life of the Church. It is new in strengthening the vocation of every member of the Church.[1] It is new in striving to close the gap between faith and the secular culture of our time; new in be-

---

[1]   John Paul II, "Toward the Fifth Centenary of New World Evangelization," *Origins*, vol. XX, No. 13, p. 215.

ing "not a matter of merely passing on doctrine but rather of a personal and profound meeting with the Savior" directed to eternal life with God.[2]

The Apostleship of Prayer is wide open to the new evangelization, for the Pope says in his encyclical, *Redemptoris Missio* [#42], that "The witness of a Christian life is the first and irreplaceable form of mission," and we Apostleship members give it. Daily we pledge Christ our hearts and our lives; we enter deep into his Heart in Eucharist and prayer; we pray for the Church and the world as the Pope directs us with his monthly intentions. Deeds more than words! Love of God in Christ above all! Genuine service flowing from love. That is why the Pope so urges the spread of devotion to the Heart of Jesus through life in the Apostleship of Prayer. Here there are no empty emotions, but a walking with Christ through thick and thin in the duties of our state of life.

You need have no fear of joining. In this League there is no human master who is going to drive you too hard. The only human Master it involves is the God-Man. Surely you trust that he will not ask you anything unreasonable or too hard for you. His Holy Spirit provides you with the strength to do whatever he asks. No other master can do that.

So now I ask you to pray the Daily Offering with me. Please pick up the Daily Offering cards in the pew and pass them to one another. We'll say the prayer together, and you'll see further what I've been explaining. Then I'll invite you to join the Apostleship of Prayer, or renew your membership. There are no dues, signatures, meetings, or obligations under sin. To join is to tell our Lord you love him enough to say and live the Daily Offering and a decade of Mary's rosary as a help to keeping your baptismal promises of loving and serving him from the heart.

Please join me in the prayer now:
"O Jesus..."
Doesn't that prayer make it evident why Pope Pius XII called

---

[2] Avery Dulles, "John Paul II and the New Evangelization," *America*, 2/1/92, pp. 52-59, 69-72; quote from p. 57.

the Apostleship "a most perfect form of Christian life"? It helps us draw close to Jesus and live close to Jesus. We fulfill our duty to be missionaries, by prayer, by witness in the world, by deep rooting in the Church and its sacramental life, by our lived hope of advancing the civilization of love, and professing faith in eternal life with God in Christ. If we can, we foster deeper devotion to his Heart by First Friday Communions of reparation, by devotion to the Immaculate Heart of Mary, and by reciting her rosary, or at least a decade each day.

I now invite you to join the Apostleship of Prayer, the League of the Heart of Jesus, or to renew your membership. I'll first say the pledge, then repeat it and invite you to say it after me:
LORD JESUS CHRIST—
I WISH TO BE A MEMBER—
OF THE APOSTLESHIP OF PRAYER.—
THE LEAGUE OF THE HEART OF JESUS.—
I PROMISE TO SAY—
AND WITH YOUR HELP TO LIVE—
THE DAILY OFFERING.
Now if you wish to join, stand and repeat after me....
NOW I ADMIT YOU AS LIFELONG MEMBERS OF THE APOS-
TLESHIP OF PRAYER, THE GREAT LEAGUE OF THE HEART OF JESUS. MEMBERSHIP IS A DRAMA OF A GREAT LEAGUE ADVANC-
ING THE KINGDOM OF GOD EVERYWHERE.

HOMILY OUTLINE

* "Everyone who acknowledges me before others...."
I. We turn from Christ's saving deeds to our response.
  * We've celebrated Easter, Pentecost, Holy Trinity, Corpus Christi and the Solemnity of the Sacred Heart.
  * Now the Readings turn to our deeds: Jeremiah's struggle, Paul's account of salvation history, Jesus' warning against losing salvation, and his calling us to witness to him and promising his witness to us before the Father.
  * Today's call is one of many calls to know him heart to Heart, share his yoke, work for the kingdom.
  * At Mass: "Thy will we done!" We need help to submit our will.

II. I offer the great help of the Apostleship of Prayer.

* Daily Offering follow up on the "Our Father": we pledge our will and lives in our state of life.
* *The Young*: You must choose state of life. Say the Daily Offering and Evening Exam and God will help you do it wisely.
* *All of Us*: The Daily Offering wins the guidance we need to live day by day for Christ and consecrates all we do.
* It makes us missionaries in prayer and action: for Church and world according to the intentions of the Heart of Christ and of the Pope.
* Daily Examen helps us make ongoing corrections.
* Apostleship of Prayer fulfills Vatican II: get involved!
* John Paul II's "new evangelization": celebrate 2000 years of Christ and his Church; close gap between faith and culture; meet Christ more personally and aim for eternal life.
* Apostleship of Prayer helps: personal witness; mission by daily pledge and living it; one with the Heart of Christ in the Eucharist, prayer, and work for the Church and the world; love in action! With Christ through all.

III. Daily Offering and the pledge to join the Apostleship of Prayer.

* Take up the Daily Offering Cards... I'll invite joining the Apostleship of Prayer.
* No dues, meetings, signatures, or obligation under sin.
* Say prayer with me now... Do you see why Pius XII calls it "a most perfect form of Christian life"? Roots us in Christ and his mission work by prayer, sacraments, action, devotion to Hearts of Jesus and Mary, rosary.
* Invitation to join: I'll say the pledge first....
  LORD JESUS CHRIST—
  I WISH TO BE A MEMBER—
  OF THE APOSTLESHIP OF PRAYER—
  THE LEAGUE OF THE SACRED HEART—
  I PROMISE TO SAY—
  AND WITH YOUR HELP TO LIVE—
  THE DAILY OFFERING.
  I NOW ADMIT YOU AS LIFELONG MEMBERS....

Membership: drama of a great League advancing kingdom worldwide.

"A" — Fourteenth Sunday in Ordinary Time   Zc 9:9-10
                                                  Rm 8:9, 11-13
                                                  Mt 11:25-31

THE EUCHARIST AND THE LEAGUE OF THE HEART OF JESUS

HOMILETIC REALIZATIONS

Many believers with ardent devotion to the Heart of Jesus head like homing pigeons to the Eucharist because Jesus' Real Presence is also the presence of his beating Heart. The truth of this statement was before our eyes in the mid-twentieth century in the great flocks of the faithful who thronged to First Friday Mass and Communion.

Pope Paul VI, lamenting the decline of this devotion, called for its restoration in *Investigabiles Divitias Christi,* a February 6, 1965 letter to the religious orders dedicated to promoting the devotion. His letter made the point that Vatican II "brought to light the brilliant mystery of the Holy Church. But this mystery can never be properly understood if the attention of the people is not drawn to that eternal love of the Incarnate Word, of which the wounded Heart of Jesus is the outstanding symbol; for, as we read in the dogmatic Constitution which bears its name, 'The Church, or, in other words, the kingdom of Christ now present in mystery, grows visibly through the power of God in the world. This inauguration and this growth are both symbolized by the blood and water which flowed from the open side of a crucified Jesus' (#3)."

The homiletic point, then: Jesus calls his people to his Heart and his Eucharist; the Magisterium does the same; the hearts of the holy feel the call in all its power. Our role in prayer and preaching is to inspire that sea of faces before us to hunger and thirst for the love of Jesus and the bread of life. If we succeed, the rest will take care of itself: their keeping of the commandments, and their eagerness for noble deeds.

PENITENTIAL RITE

To prepare ourselves to celebrate these sacred mysteries of the body and blood of Christ, let us call to mind our sins against the threefold command of love: the love of God above all things; the love of our neighbor as ourselves; and the love of one another as Christ has loved us.

THE EUCHARIST AND THE LEAGUE OF THE HEART OF JESUS

"Come to me... and learn from me, for I am meek and humble of heart; and you will find rest for yourselves."

Where can we possibly find rest of the kind that Jesus is speaking about, the kind that will last and endure always? Where, except in love? Not in love on the rush, but in love at home, in the Heart of God, love and rest that will last forever.

Do you recognize, then, this call for what it is, the call of love, and the call to love, from Almighty God himself, God in the flesh, born of the Virgin Mary in the stable on the high hills of Bethlehem in the piercing cold of winter?

This invitation of Jesus contains many invitations and ways of his coming to us and our coming to him, but he has given us no other way as profound as the Mass and the Eucharist.

The Eucharist is the greatest mystery of love the world has ever seen. It is Jesus' own Sacrament of Love. It could only be given by a God who has become Man. We begin to receive it on earth, but it is so great it is one of God's earth-time gifts that will continue in heaven, as the Council of Trent taught.

God calls us to a total self-giving to him, one compared to which the self-giving in human marriage is a lesser imitation. That is why the Scriptures portray the Church giving itself as a bridal gift to Christ to return his great love. This is biblical, mystical language, used by God to speak of his inexpressible relationship to his people.

Today I will invite you to return the Eucharistic love of Jesus

more actively day in and day out through the practices of the
Apostleship of Prayer, the League of the Heart of Jesus. For true love
must be expressed in works as well as words and feelings. I remind
you of how many speak of love and how few of the works of love, and
of how God speaks of the works of love from the first pages of the
Bible to the last.

Did you notice how Jesus called us to share his love in an active way by sharing his work as well? "Take my yoke upon you and
learn from me," he said, "for I am meek and humble of heart." As a
carpenter Jesus must often have made a yoke and seen two oxen
yoked with it pulling one load. We're called to share Jesus' yoke and
pull his load with him.

To his call in words Jesus crucified added the call of his pierced
Heart, opened for us. In the water that flowed out we and the Church
were born in baptism; in the blood we are nourished by the Eucharist. As the Fathers of the Church taught, the symbolism of Eve being born from the side of Adam was fulfilled in Christ on the cross.
The last Adam, Christ crucified, gave birth to the new Eve, the
Church.

Jesus himself sped up the pace of the spread of the devotion to
his Heart some 300 years ago. In a series of visions closely connected
with the Eucharist, he appeared to St. Margaret Mary. He showed
her his wounded Heart with warm and brilliant flames of love shoot-
ing out. He told her that if he had not given us the Sacrament of his
Love, he would have given it to her personally because she so longed
for it. Could he say that to you?

Once, the Blessed Mother appeared to her, and spoke of how
people must be told of the benefits they can receive from this Heart
if they come with respect and gratitude.

St. Margaret was so fired up she said, "If people knew how
pleasing this devotion is to Jesus Christ, there wouldn't be a Christian with so little love for this lovable Savior as not to embrace it at
once." Is that true of you?

To spread the devotion to his divine Heart and win salvation
for uncounted numbers of people, zealous priests founded the

Apostleship of Prayer, the League of the Heart of Jesus, and spread the Devotion. Pope after Pope has urged us to respond. Pope Paul VI said, "The Church was born from the pierced heart of the Redeemer, and is nourished there.... Thus it is absolutely necessary that the faithful venerate and honor this Heart" (Letter of May 25, 1965). And in his April 13, 1985 address to the National Secretaries of the Apostleship of Prayer, Pope John Paul II said: "I put this worldwide Pious Association into your hands as a precious treasure from the Pope's heart and the Heart of Christ."

What, then, is this wonderful Apostleship of Prayer? It is the League of the Heart of Jesus, a union of tens of millions of us Catholics from little children to the Pope who band together to say and live the Daily Offering. We offer Jesus our every action in union with the Holy Sacrifice of the Mass to help bring his kingdom, which is also ours.

You will find the Daily Offering cards in the pews. Hand them to one another, and say the Daily Offering with me now....

(After saying the prayer, invite the people to pocket the card.)

By that little prayer we offer the Lord all we are and do, and become more consciously a part of his apostolic team. That little prayer is at the heart of the Church. It helps us find the meaning of life by serving the Heart of our Redeemer. It helps us fulfill our baptism by putting to use our baptismal share in Christ's kingship, priesthood, and prophetic mission.

What I want to do next is explain the Daily Offering's relationship to the Mass and Holy Communion.

Christ became Man to restore all creation to the Father, and his call to us to help him is expressed not only in today's Gospel but even in the Eucharistic symbolism of the unleavened bread and the cup of his blood. The unleavened bread recalls the journey of the Chosen People from the slavery of Egypt to the promised land. Called suddenly to that journey of freedom, they took with them the dough to make their bread, without having time to leaven it. Christ chose unleavened bread for the Eucharist to tell us we too are called to make the journey of life to freedom in the promised land of heaven. We don't have time to get involved in the materialism that surrounds us. We must remain free to walk the way of Christ.

Before the Chosen People left Egypt, they put the blood of the paschal lamb on their doorposts. It signaled to the angel of death that he should leave them unhurt when he passed by to execute judgment on their slave drivers. The Eucharistic blood of Christ the new Paschal Lamb marks the doorposts of our lips with the sign that we are to be freed from judgment. We have passed into life everlasting if only we remain faithful.

When the Jewish people went forth to freedom they were fed by the manna from heaven. We are fed the true Bread from heaven, the risen, immortal body and blood of Christ. It is our Food for the journey.

What are the consequences of all this? We the Church are the new Eve, born from the side of the last Adam, through the sacrifice of Calvary and the mystery of the pierced Heart of Jesus renewed in the sacrifice of the Mass. We come from Christ and belong to Christ, as Christ belongs to God. We give to Christ as he gives to us. His gift is himself, and our gift is ourselves. It includes all we are and do. We express that in the Daily Offering.

That is why our Apostleship of Prayer's practice of devotion to the Heart of Jesus is Eucharistic.

In the Daily Offering we unite everything with the Mass. All we think, do and say is put on the paten with Christ at every Mass around the world even as we're doing it. It is also united with Holy Communion, for like the branches of a vine, we are extensions of the body of Christ, and he is at work in us 24 hours a day.

We do everything in the spirit of reparation. Reparation is a profound religious word, but basically it means "to repair." When something breaks we repair it. Sin broke God's world, and Christ offered himself on Calvary and in the Mass as an atoning sacrifice, a repairing. We join Christ crucified in repairing the world and redeeming sinners by prayers, works, joys and sufferings, all done in accord with God's will. Our good deeds of obedience to the Father atone for sinful ones and for the good ones left undone.

Pope John Paul II explained that "the true meaning of reparation demanded by the Heart of the Savior" is to learn from the Heart of Christ "the true and only meaning of life," and on the ruins of hatred and violence to build the "civilization of love," "the Kingdom of the Heart of Christ" (Letter of 12/5/86 to Director General of the A.P.). Who does not want to be part of this noblest of all enterprises rather than build his own shabby little kingdom which must soon fade away?

Christ, in his revelations to St. Margaret Mary, called especially for a monthly Holy Hour and Communion of Reparation. He kept the devotion to his Heart centered on his Eucharistic Sacrifice and presence. For the Eucharist is the Sacrament of Love, and devotion to his Heart calls for a burning love that withholds nothing from him who gave everything.

I will now summarize and invite you to enroll in the Apostleship of Prayer. In summary, then: The heart of our religion is that God became flesh—the Incarnation. The heart of the Incarnation is the Heart of Jesus. In his Heart the Church lives and breathes. We give a central role to Mary his Mother, and say at least a decade of her rosary daily. We love the Church as his creation, and obey the Holy Father and the bishops.

Our Lord chose to come and become Man in the immaculate womb of Mary his Mother. We return everything through her Immaculate Heart. What could please him more? We go to her as our Mother and special intercessor. We imitate her, the most loving, noble, sinless, zealous comrade, apostle, disciple and servant of Jesus and lover of the Eucharist the world has ever seen. We draw close to her, and we say at least a decade of her rosary every day.

We love the Church as Christ's creation and her teaching as his own. We live and breathe the Church. It is the body of Christ where we have eternal life. We love and honor the Holy Father. We say our Daily Offering as part of his prayer team, and include the special intention he gives us to pray for each month.

I now invite you to join the Apostleship of Prayer. First, I'll say the pledge so you know what you're pledging, then ask you to stand and repeat it loud and clear.

LORD JESUS CHRIST—
I WISH TO BE A MEMBER—
OF THE APOSTLESHIP OF PRAYER—
THE LEAGUE OF THE HEART OF JESUS.—
I PROMISE TO SAY—
AND WITH YOUR HELP TO LIVE—
THE DAILY OFFERING.
          I NOW ADMIT YOU AS LIFELONG MEMBERS OF THE APOS-
TLESHIP OF PRAYER, THE LEAGUE OF THE HEART OF JESUS.

HOMILY OUTLINE

* "Come to me... and learn from me, for I am meek and humble of heart; and you will find rest for yourselves."
* Where find enduring rest, except in love, at home in God.
* Do you recognize his words as the call to love?
I. This Invitation contains many invitations, but above all to Mass and Holy Communion, the greatest mystery of love
* Only God can give it: a gift for earth and heaven.
* Our response must be total: greater than in marriage.
* I'll invite response via Apostleship of Prayer and the Heart of Jesus Devotion.
* Jesus calls us to "yoke" ourselves to him: love in deeds, at work with him.
* He adds the call of his pierced Heart: its symbolism.
* His calls through St. Margaret Mary: their content.
* Why the Apostleship of Prayer was founded; why Popes urge us to join.
* What the Apostleship of Prayer and the League of the Heart of Jesus is.
* Say the Daily Offering with me....
* That daily prayer helps us use kingly, priestly, prophetic gifts.
II. I'll explain the Daily Offering's relationship to Mass and Holy Communion.
* Christ became man to restore fallen creation to the Father.
* By symbols he enlists our help: yoke, unleavened bread, blood on our lips, bread from heaven.

* Consequences: we, the Church, the new Eve, from pierced side via Calvary/Mass; as he gives all, so we in return: Daily Offering promises it.

III. Thus the A.P. Devotion to Heart of Jesus is Eucharistic.

* Everything on the paten with Christ even as we live our day.
* Everything offered in the spirit of reparation: we repair with Christ crucified; John Paul II's explanation of reparation.
* Mass, Holy Communion, Holy Hour, First Fridays, good actions: all repair and upbuild and restore and elevate creation.
* *Summary and Enrollment*: Incarnation; via Immaculate womb of Mary; we return via Immaculate Heart of Mary; we live and breathe Church; join in prayer of Holy Father for Church.
* *Enrollment*:

LORD JESUS CHRIST—

I WISH TO BE A MEMBER—

OF THE APOSTLESHIP OF PRAYER—

THE LEAGUE OF THE HEART OF JESUS—

I PROMISE TO SAY—

AND WITH YOUR HELP TO LIVE—

THE DAILY OFFERING.

I NOW ADMIT YOU AS LIFELONG MEMBERS OF THE APOSTLESHIP OF PRAYER, THE LEAGUE OF THE HEART OF JESUS.

Adaptation to Holy Hour, Forty Hours

This homily can be so adapted simply by using the Gospel reading from the "A"— Fourteenth Sunday in Ordinary Time for the services listed.

"C" — Seventeenth Sunday in Ordinary Time   Gn 18:20-32
                                                   Col 2:12-14
                                                   Lk 11:1-13

THE LEAGUE THAT TEACHES PRAYER

HOMILETIC REALIZATIONS

Are any of us ever satisfied we have done enough to teach our people prayer? In learning to pray, and in teaching to pray, the rule seems to be: "We all need all the help we can get."

If, then, to the help Jesus gives in today's Gospel, our homily adds something of the help his Holy Spirit has given the Church through St. Ignatius of Loyola and the Apostleship of Prayer, it will be a praiseworthy service to the congregation.

Far more helpful than generalities about prayer is an introduction to a simple method of prayer, and an inducement to make a commitment to an enduring practice of prayer. These two things can help people grow not for a day but for a lifetime.

Why, then, not take Jesus' teaching on prayer as an opportunity to introduce St. Ignatius' simple but profound "Second Method of Prayer," a form of genuine mental prayer? And, since the Ignatian system of prayer inspired the founding, and informs the practices, of the Apostleship of Prayer, why not illustrate the second method of prayer by a prayerful instructive meditation on the Daily Offering? (One can fully appreciate the value of this only by realizing that the Daily Offering captures much of the fruit of the Kingdom Meditation, which is so central to Ignatius's *Spiritual Exercises*). And why not follow up by inviting people to join the Apostleship of Prayer? Or to renew membership, for we need to be mindful that some parishioners almost certainly did not join at prior opportunities, others did but have fallen away, and some were not even present.

In the Gospel, the Son of God invites us to ask for what we

want, for our Father is a giving Father. Isn't this Sunday, then, a splendid chance to point out that by saying and living the Daily Offering, we delight God by giving instead of asking! That's the beauty, the value of the Apostleship of Prayer.

Any day our homily wins one more person to a lifelong practice of saying and living the Daily Offering, the Holy Spirit has blessed our efforts. And we can surely hope we will win many more than one. So on to the task, then, of teaching prayer.

SUGGESTED PENITENTIAL RITE

To prepare ourselves to offer this Holy Sacrifice let us individually call to mind our sins. Today let us inspect in particular whether we have neglected Jesus' call to pray always, letting hours and days go by without praying. Have we, perhaps, failed even to ask our Father for the graces we need to avoid evil and do good, as Jesus taught us? So let us examine ourselves, then we will appeal collectively to our saving Lord, who poured out those sacred streams from his pierced side to wash away our sins and redeem us.

(Continue with the formula: "Lord Jesus, you are mighty God...")

THE LEAGUE THAT TEACHES PRAYER

"Lord, teach us to pray."

Today let us make that plea our own, for it is one of the most needed and most enriching of all God's gifts. In response to his disciples' request, Jesus taught us the "Our Father," that incomparable prayer to the Father. Today I will offer an instruction in a form of mental prayer that I ask you to apply to the "Our Father" at home; here I will explain it by applying it to a prayer to Jesus, the Daily Offering of the Apostleship of Prayer. The reason for my choice is that I want to invite you to join or renew your membership in the Apostleship of Prayer—the "A.P." for short.

But first, I want to show the relationship of prayer to happiness.

"What can bring us happiness?" Psalm 4 asks. What indeed? How can we find happiness? How can we invite it into our lives?

Hear the answer of one famous man: "I really do not think there is any person much unhappier than I," he declared. I am quoting Benjamin Disraeli, the English Prime Minister of a century ago. Reflecting on his unhappiness, Disraeli said, "Fortune, fashion, fame, even power, may increase and do heighten happiness, but they do not create it. Happiness can spring only from the affections."

He knew what he was talking about. He had fortune, fame and power, but he was unhappy because the passing of the years had taken from him all his loved ones. Happiness arises from the heart; an unhappy heart is an unhappy person.

The Lord alone brings us ever-enduring happiness. He will always love us and he alone will never leave us. Only he can show us "the path to life," and bring us into "the delights at (his) right hand forever" (Ps 16).

When you ask, "What can bring us happiness?", do you hear the answer ringing out in the call of Jesus, "Come to me, all you who labor and are burdened, and I will give you rest. Take my yoke upon you and learn from me, for I am meek and humble of heart; and you will find rest for yourselves. For my yoke is easy, my burden light" (Mt 11:29)?

His call profits us only if we answer it with our hearts and with our backs by sharing his yoke in the labors and adventures that lead to eternal glory.

Mary answered as his mother. Joseph answered as his foster-father, head of the house and support of the family. We must imitate them and imitate Jesus himself. Jesus set us an example as an obedient Son, a worker who earned a living as a carpenter, and a laborer in the vineyard of the work for the redemption of the world. Whatever our state or station in life, we are to imitate them.

To assist you in doing that, I invite you to join or renew your membership in the Apostleship of Prayer, the League of the Heart of Jesus.

This is a tried and true way of returning Jesus love for love.

At the ends of the pews you'll find Daily Offering cards. Please distribute them to one another, and say the prayer with me. Then I'll meditate on it aloud in a form of mental prayer that can enrich your prayer life. Joining the A.P. requires no dues, signatures, meetings, or obligations under sin. It's a promise of love to be lived always. By daily saying and living the Daily Offering, we daily renew our self-giving to Jesus, and we say at least a decade of Our Blessed Mother's rosary.

Please kneel now, and pray with me:

"O Jesus, through...."

Please be seated—and pocket your card. You can see this is a prayer which unites our hearts with the Heart of Jesus and all his concerns.

Since Jesus taught the "Our Father," his Holy Spirit has taught the Church many ways to pray, and using the Daily Offering, I will provide a brief instruction in what is called Mental Prayer.

The method I'll present, taken from St. Ignatius, is called "The Second Method of Prayer." It's simple but profound. It can lead to great depths of prayer, as St. Teresa of Avila showed in her mystical writings.

Please join me in spirit as I meditate aloud on the Morning Offering. Because of limited time, I won't try to get to the end of it, and that is O.K. when you use it too. Let me begin, then.

Lord, I put myself in your presence, for you said you would be with us always. I begin my prayer in your company.

"O Jesus." Jesus, what a wealth of truth and love and revelation your name brings to mind and heart. Your name was owned by other newborns before you in the history of your people. It is through our Lady's ears that we first hear of it belonging to you. O Mary, Virgin of Nazareth, we remember how the angel Gabriel announced to you that your Son would be conceived in your womb; that he would be born of you and be called Jesus; and that you must know he is the Son of the Most High.

Jesus, Son of God, from the beginning you were the Word, and were with God, and were God. You became flesh of the Virgin Mary, and dwelt among us.

Jesus, true God and true Man, you had a Heart like ours. It warmed with love for your friends; it beat with fear in the agony in the Garden. Your Heart had all the experiences of ours, except that of sin. You came the sinless One to take away the sins of the world.

"O Jesus, through the Immaculate Heart of Mary." Through her immaculate womb you came to us. Through her Immaculate Heart, if she allows me, I come to you. How could I please you more? How more surely come to you?

Every time I offer you the gift of my daily life, Our Lady brushes away the chaff and gives you only the wheat. How happy it must make you to receive all through her tender, loving maternal, Immaculate Heart.

Mary, Jesus on the cross made you our Mother. Help us daily say and live this prayer of love to the Heart of your Son.

"Through the Immaculate Heart of Mary I offer you...." Jesus, you offered yourself for us. How can I ever return a worthy offering when I remember you are God, infinitely beyond me? The thought of exchanging love with you makes me feel so inadequate.

Then I think of little children. A little child is completely dependent and trusting, and loves spontaneously. Rising up on the bridge of love, he forgets all differences, and meets as friend with friend, though the other be God himself. That helps me understand why you said, "Unless you turn and become like children, you will not enter the kingdom of heaven."

You teach us to be as simple as children with you, Lord Jesus. You give us your Heart, and want ours. All distances and all differences, even that between the divine and the human, are forgotten. You acted to close all distances by becoming human, and then you made it possible for us to be called children of God by giving us a share in your divine Sonship through baptism.

"I offer you all my prayers, works, joys and sufferings." I offer you everything, Lord, for all the intentions of your Sacred Heart. I offer you my life and my living of it.

I offer it **"...in union with the Holy Sacrifice of the Mass throughout the world."** How privileged I feel, Jesus, to have my thoughts, words and deeds on the paten with you at every Mass offered as I live them out. I offer them now and always. Amen.

I hope you see how simple it is to make this prayer from the heart. I hope you will use this method when you pray the "Our Father," the "Hail Mary," and the "Daily Offering" yourself, and also on loved passages of Scripture, as I do.

So now I invite you to join the Apostleship of Prayer, the League of the Heart of Jesus. All you pledge is to say the Daily Offering and try to live it, and to say at least a decade of our Lady's rosary each day. I'll first read the pledge for you to hear, then invite you to make or renew the consecration. Here is the pledge:

LORD JESUS CHRIST—
I WISH TO BE A MEMBER—
OF THE APOSTLESHIP OF PRAYER—
THE LEAGUE OF THE HEART OF JESUS.—
I PROMISE TO SAY—
AND WITH YOUR HELP TO LIVE—
THE DAILY OFFERING.

If you'd like to join, stand now and repeat after me....

I NOW ENROLL YOU OR RENEW YOUR ENROLLMENT IN THE APOSTLESHIP OF PRAYER, THE LEAGUE OF THE HEART OF JESUS.

We're tens of millions strong around the world, trying to make this the civilization of love, the Kingdom of the Heart of Christ.

HOMILY OUTLINE:

* "Lord, teach us to pray."
* Let's make this plea ours. Jesus' answer; my intention here: to teach mental prayer and apply it to the Daily Offering—and why.

I. First, a look at the relationship between prayer and happiness.

    * "What can bring us happiness?" Psalm 4 asks. We all ask that.
    * Answer of one famous man: English Prime Minister Benjamin Disraeli: He knew—*He had all of the above!*
    * Only the Lord can give us secure happiness: He'll always love us, never leave us, and he will guide us to happiness here and hereafter.
    * Happiness? Hear the call of Jesus: "Come to me...."
    * The happiness of being his loving companion in labor, adventure and glory.
    * Of profit only if we answer—as Mary did..., as Joseph did.
    * We imitate Jesus, obedient Son, carpenter, Savior.

II. To help you I invite you to join the Apostleship of Prayer, the League of the Sacred Heart.

    * Take up cards... no dues, signatures, obligation under sin.
    * Pray the Daily Offering with me now... (pocket card).

III. Teaching on Mental Prayer, using Daily Offering

    * Join me in spirit as I meditate aloud:
    * *"O Jesus"*: owned by others....
    * Mary, through your ears we hear Gabriel....
    * Son of God/Word—you became flesh; true God/Man;
    * Heart like ours; experiences like ours....
    * *"Through the Immaculate Heart of Mary"*—you came via her Immaculate Womb.
    * I return via her Immaculate Heart. How please you more?
    * I offer daily; she brushes away the chaff....
    * *"Through the IHM, I offer"*: How return your love? Ridiculous?
    * Answer: little children, etc.
    * Your Incarnation and our adoption closed gap.
    * *"I offer you all my prayers, works, joys, sufferings."*— even my life.
    * *"In union with the Holy Sacrifice of the Mass...."* What a privilege!
    * See how good and simple this is; use it on "Our Father," "Hail Mary," etc.

* *Invitation to join the AP/League*: just say and live Daily Offering plus a decade of the rosary.

Enrollment (Plenary Indulgence):

> LORD JESUS CHRIST—
> I WISH TO BE A MEMBER—
> OF THE APOSTLESHIP OF PRAYER—
> I PROMISE TO SAY—
> AND WITH YOUR HELP TO LIVE—
> THE DAILY OFFERING.

I NOW ENROLL YOU OR RENEW YOUR ENROLLMENT IN THE APOSTLESHIP OF PRAYER, THE LEAGUE OF THE HEART OF JESUS, THE LEAGUE OF THE CIVILIZATION OF LOVE, THE KINGDOM OF THE HEART OF CHRIST.

This homily can be readily adapted to other Sundays, especially Sundays in which the Gospel deals with prayer, by changing the homily's opening Gospel quote and first paragraph.

Chapter Five

TO JESUS' HEART
THROUGH THE *OUR FATHER*

Homilies For
A HEART OF JESUS NOVENA ON THE *OUR FATHER*

FIRST DAY

THE PRAYER OF PRAYERS

HOMILETIC REALIZATIONS

Years ago, in a talk on Sacred Heart Radio entitled "New Life for the 'Our Father'," I began with two questions: Is there any way to revitalize prayers we repeatedly say? How can we break the habit of rattling off these prayers without attention or devotion?

My answer was that there is a way; that everything, even the "Our Father," needs care and maintenance, as a plant needs rain. We give the "Our Father" care by giving it the dew and rain of meditation on each word and phrase.

The *Catechism of the Catholic Church* resoundingly affirms this need, for "Jesus did not give us a formula to repeat mechanically," but "he gives us the Spirit by whom these words become in us 'spirit and life'" (#2766). And so the *Catechism* itself proceeds to provide the doctrine for a profound meditation on the "Our Father."

The homilies in a Novena dedicated to the Heart of Jesus should help us grow in knowledge of his Heart, and in the ways of prayer so that we can commune with his Heart. In a letter to the Director General of the Apostleship of Prayer, Pope John Paul II described with forceful brevity how that can be done: "The more one learns to inspire one's own prayer with the word of God, the more intimately that person is permeated with the sentiments of the Heart of Christ. In this way participation in the liturgical life becomes extraordinarily effective. It will be the task of the Apostleship of Prayer to promote this lively participation, fully aware of its essential importance for the success of the new evangelization.

"The new evangelization will also be effective insofar as it strengthens the bonds of ecclesial communion with the grace that flows from the Heart of Christ."[1]

---

[1] *L'Osservatore Romano*, Dec. 21/28, 1994, p. 7.

The word of God, the word of Christ, and the prayer of the
Heart of Christ coalesce in the Our Father. It is an immensely rich
place to mine. With it as our source, we can help the faithful make
progress in going from knowing about Jesus to knowing Jesus as he
knows them. If done prayerfully it brings us heart to heart with Jesus.
Our homilies in this Novena should inspire those present to continue
lifelong their mining of the "Our Father," that treasure of revelation
of the Heart of Jesus.

Since the nine homilies that follow all take their source from the
"Our Father," this single homiletic reflection will serve for them all.
And since the homilies here are more simple than those in preced-
ing chapters, they are not followed up by an outline.

THE PRAYER OF PRAYERS

**Dear friends in the Lord, join me in calling to mind
Jacob's well as a symbol of our hearts.**

Recall that it is where Jesus asked the Samaritan woman for a
drink, and told her he'd have given her living water if she'd asked him
(Jn 4:4-42). In confusion, she replied, "Sir, this well is deep and you
don't have a bucket."

If ever you visit the Holy Land, you will find that to this day
Jacob's well provides thirsty travelers with a drink. But it is very deep.
One must lower a bucket far down and draw it up with rope and
winch.

Our hearts are like that. Our holy longings and desires are so
deep down that at times when we try to speak to God about them we
are unable to draw them up to give him the drink he desires of us.

**What if there were a prayer which could help us bring to
our lips all we most want to say, a prayer placing before God
in one brief burst our deepest thoughts and loving desires?**

There is such a prayer, of course: the "Our Father" which Jesus
taught us. It is the inexhaustible prayer I will pray and ponder over
with you during this Heart of Jesus Novena.

Right here, in the heart of this homily, please kneel and say the prayer with me now:

Our Father, who art in heaven, hallowed be thy name. Thy kingdom come, thy will be done on earth as it is in heaven. Give us this day our daily bread and forgive us our trespasses, as we forgive those who trespass against us. Lead us not into temptation, but deliver us from evil. Amen.

With the "Our Father" fresh in mind serving as guide, let's ask ourselves what our deepest thoughts and profoundest desires are. Let's reach down into our heart's deep well and bring them up one by one.

Isn't the first one that comes up the desire to honor God and see him honored by all? Don't we weary of neglecting him, and grieve at the neglect of others which gives such a sordid turn to world affairs?

Let's lower our spiritual bucket again. Now I see coming up the desire for the return of paradise—of God's kingdom on earth—of innocence and happiness and joy on all faces, and of life lived in the presence of God.

Up comes our bucket again. Swimming in it are the pure waters of desire to put aside our wayward pursuits and do God's will, and see it done by all. For God's will alone is unsullied by selfishness and lighted by all that is wise and good. His will alone can restore his kingdom on earth.

And now, coming up in our bucket is the desire for the fulfillment of our simple daily wants uncluttered by inflated needs. We see what's really necessary—the spiritual and bodily food, drink and shelter that our Lord was satisfied with when he pitched his tent among us.

Once again we lower our bucket. Rising into view is the draft of peace, the desire of every living heart. We long to have peace in us and around us, to possess it within our hearts and experience it with our neighbors. "If only we could get along together," we think; "forgive and be forgiven; forget the past and look to the future. O, for reconciliation between God and man, neighbor and neighbor, nation and nation."

We speak plaintively, speak with our "If only"—yet we know, in our deepest hearts, that we should speak not with "if" but with "when." Are we not aware that when we really desire it, we can have peace? For the Prince of Peace came to bring peace, and left his peace with us for the using. At the Last Supper he said, "Peace is my farewell to you, my peace is my gift to you" (Jn 15:27). Peace is a reality into which we must put not our "ifs" but our backs. It is not a wish but a work.

It is a work of justice and love, forgiveness and giving. Peace is possible. When we wash one another's feet as Jesus did, we find it. And once we find it, no man can take it from us. For "his will is our peace," and the two, having been joined by God, cannot be separated by man. In the heart that does his will, there is peace.

One last time the bucket goes down. Up it comes, sparkling with longing for self-respect and self-esteem. We want to be good— persons who have broken with evil, men and women and children eager for noble deeds. Who of us hasn't felt our heart soar as we sat engrossed in some tale of hero and heroine triumphing over every temptation, overcoming every obstacle, and walking into the future with unsullied heart?

These, then, are surely the deepest desires of our hearts, we who are friends of God. It is of these things that we long to speak to God in prayer. And the amazing prayer Jesus taught us draws up these very thoughts and desires from our hearts and puts them on our lips in a matter of minutes.

Our privileged and prayerful work during this Novena of the Heart of Jesus will be to gaze by means of these words he gave us into the Heart of Jesus from which they came.

Tomorrow we will begin searching out not simply what the "Our Father" means, but how we can live it like Jesus did. That is the true route by which we can travel into his Heart, for by giving us the "Our Father" to pray and to live, he has opened his Heart to all who wish to enter it.

I'm talking about a great mystery—the mystery not of coming to know about Jesus, but of coming to know Jesus; the mystery not of just knowing Jesus but of so coming to share his life that he says, "I am the vine and you the branches."

The *Catechism of the Catholic Church* (#2767) tells us that the early Christians prayed the "Our Father" three times daily in place of the "Eighteen Benedictions" of Jewish piety. So let us now, with great interior recollection and piety, kneel and say the prayer again, and go home to meditate on it through the day until we come together tomorrow.

Our Father, who art in heaven, hallowed be thy name. Thy kingdom come, thy will be done on earth as it is in heaven. Give us this day our daily bread and forgive us our trespasses, as we forgive those who trespass against us. Lead us not into temptation, but deliver us from evil. Amen.

WHERE JESUS OPENED HIS HEART

Dear friends in the Lord, when do we most open our hearts? Isn't it in prayer, since God knows all anyhow? But there's another time, too, which we haven't experienced yet: on our deathbeds. Dying people take that last chance to tell their loved ones what is most in their hearts.

On the deathbed of his cross, Jesus opened his heart in the seven last words. But all his life he opened his Heart to his Father in prayer. **Jesus prayed much. If only we could listen in! Did he give us a way to do it?**

I believe he did. We know that when the disciples asked him to teach them to pray, he gave them and us the very prayer around which we are making our novena, the "Our Father." Wouldn't he cram that one prayer he taught us with the things in all his prayers which were dearest to his Heart? He'd make it a kind of *listening in prayer*, full of his love, devotion and petitions to the Father for us and our world.

That Jesus did just that is shown by the fact that the "Our Father" is so filled with the treasures of his Heart that after 2000 years his Church still finds it inexhaustible. That is because by entering deep into the "Our Father" we enter deep into the Heart of Jesus.

Some individuals seem to labor under the false impression that they know all about the "Our Father," but they never really do.

The Church has found much there in 2000 years, but there's always more to find. So, once more, we try to go deeper.

"Our Father who art in heaven...." The very first phrase is a revelation and a permission. We dare to say "Our Father." Through the ages most people never dared to call God "Father." He was their Almighty—and fearsome—Creator, to be obeyed and served.

Some 300 years before Christ, the brilliant pagan philosopher Aristotle said we can't even be friends of God because such is the gulf between God and us there's no common ground for friendship. Was Aristotle wrong? The Chosen People called God the Father of the people as a whole, but very rarely did an individual Jew dare to call God "Father."

Why then call God our Father? We go to Jesus for the answer.

We won't find it in mere words. We find it in the very being and identity of Jesus, and in the great deeds he did that changed the reality, deeds that made God our Father. It is to those things we need to look to learn why we call God our Father.

He, the Son of God, became Man, conceived in the womb of the Virgin. From that moment he is Son of God and Son of Mary. He is one Person in two natures, one Divine and one human. He closes the gap between humanity and divinity in his own person. And so he, a man, necessarily calls God *Father*. As the *Catechism of the Catholic Church* observes, quoting Tertullian, "The expression God the Father had never been revealed to anyone.... The Father's name has been revealed to us in the Son, for the name 'Son' implies the new name 'Father'" (#2779).

That was only the beginning. By his life and death he redeemed us. Through baptism and the Eucharist he communicates to us a share in his life and Sonship. Now we really are God's children, and God is our Father.

We call God our Father, then, because Christ has changed reality, changed our identity. He made us the Father's children not just by words of adoption and some legal contract, but by making us share his life.

Every good father is a whole environment and climate. He gives his children life, lives with them, and provides shelter and food. He guides their conduct and forms their values.

We need, too, to attend to the fact that Jesus taught us to call God "our" Father, not just "my" Father. He is calling us to pray for the whole of humanity, to whom he sent us to preach the Gospel, so that all may be reborn as the children of God, as we were. He has made the "Our Father" a missionary prayer, with us as the missionaries of prayer (See CCC, #2793).

God the Father does these things for us. He gives us life from the pierced Heart of his Son. The water from his side gives us new life by baptism. His blood is given us together with his body as our food and drink. The Father clothes us in his Son. "Put on Christ," says St. Paul.

The Father lives with us. "Whoever loves me will keep my word," Jesus said, "and my Father will love him, and we will come to him and make our dwelling with him."

By Jesus's teaching and example and Holy Spirit and Church, the Father guides us, forms our values, confirms our resolves, and never abandons us.

By praying over what Jesus has done for us, and living it, we share with Jesus the sentiments of his Heart as Son of God. How can we better pray the "Our Father" than by entering the Heart of Jesus? By practicing the devotion to the Heart of Jesus, we enter his Heart. We find him adoring the Father, and join in by saying the "Our Father" with the help of the Holy Spirit. Let us conclude this meditation by saying together right now the prayer Jesus taught us:

"Our Father...."

THIRD DAY

HALLOWING THE FATHER'S NAME

"Our Father who art in heaven, hallowed be thy name...." Since the Son of God made us the Father's children by taking us up into his very Person through baptism, we are faced with the question, How are we to live as the Father's children?

Jesus told us how when he opened his Heart to us in the "Our Father." We are to hallow the Father's name.

How do we go about hallowing the Father's name? In prayer, certainly, as Jesus did. But like Jesus, we must go from word to deed. To hallow the Father means to love and reverence and serve him as all-holy, sacred beyond our understanding.

Reverence is closely related to love. It is experienced by couples who fall deeply in love. Early on they feel a profound, even an unearthly, sense of reverence for one another. Each feels utterly unworthy of the other, feels blessed beyond hope in having love returned.

What, then, should be our reverence for God, who *is* Love? When Scripture says, "Fear of God is the beginning of wisdom," it is calling us to this sense of reverence and awe before the Father's mystery, this deep respect for God and his goodness, power and wise law.

But like Moses we have to learn reverence and cultivate it. When Moses saw the burning bush he wanted to stroll over and have a look. But God said, "Come no nearer! Remove the sandals from your feet, for the place where you stand is holy ground" (Ex 3:5).

What actions then do we have to engage in to hallow the Father's name?

We have to live as God's true children in Christ's likeness, body and soul, in everything.

The world besmirches the Father's name by corrupting his gifts thorough disbelief and sin. "The foolish son," says the Book of Proverbs, "is ruin to his father" (Pr 19:13). The history of sin besmirched the Father's name, from the fallen angels through Adam and Eve down to the latest sinner. It got so bad God the Father said, "I am sorry that I made them" (Gn 6:7-8).

Jesus came to reverse that besmirching. "Be perfect, just as your heavenly Father is perfect" (Mt 5:48). In the same vein, St. Paul declares that God the Father "chose us in him, before the foundation of the world, to be holy and without blemish before him" (Eph 1:4). That is how we hallow the Father's name.

Jesus set the pattern for us. Jesus's human nature was like ours in every way except sin.

We can't deny that truth, lest we deny he redeemed us. Pope Pius XII, insisting on this in *Haurietis Aquas,* quotes St. John Damascene, "For what was not assumed could not be healed" (#59). The pattern which Jesus gave us is consecration to God and his purposes. "My food," he said, "is to do the will of the One who sent me and to finish his work" (Jn 4:34).

Since by our baptism we, too, are consecrated to God, think of what it means by considering this parable. A woman goes to the rectory on hearing the priest needs help after flooding from a recent storm. Shocked, she discovers him using his consecrated chalice to bail out the filthy water.

Is not God, too, shocked by people who by sin degrade the image of himself in which he made them, and the image of Christ in which he remade them by baptism? Our bodies are the living ciborium and chalice into which Christ enters body and blood in Holy Communion.

"Heart of Jesus, Fountain of Life and Holiness," we pray, "have mercy on us." Pour your graces into us so we can hallow the Father's name by living like you.

Reverence is meant to be eternal. Many lose their reverence. They begin well, then take what they consider their familiarity with God as a license for irreverence. As the Saints teach us, however, such conduct comes not from familiarity with God, but from routine religious habits that lose close contact with God.

Reverence grows as familiarity with God grows. Long-married couples deeply in love manifest both reverence and familiarity for one another. As the distance between them vanishes, their respect for one another increases. That is the pattern for our hallowing of the Father's name, and we see it in Jesus. Who reverenced the Father more than Jesus?

FOURTH DAY

BUILDING THE FATHER'S KINGDOM

"Thy kingdom come, thy will be done on earth as it is in heaven." With what passion Jesus must have prayed those words!

We know with what passion he lived them. He worked all day and often prayed part of the night. At times he and his disciples were too busy to eat.

Continuing to enter Jesus's Heart through the "Our Father," we have come to this petition, and it is not hard to discover the source of the passion behind it. Jesus Christ came into a world created by his beloved Father to be a paradise and Jesus found a wasteland, a death-camp polluted by sin, the greatest environmental hazard of all time. He knew that sin would expand the pollution into every realm of nature as time went by. This was inevitable, for it is greed and selfishness and the dullness of heart they generate that incite the conduct which produces chemical contamination, radioactive pollution, and other wastes. And so he labored with all his might to undo sin because he knew that our salvation is at stake.

The Father's kingdom began to show its fullness when Jesus preached the Beatitudes as its code: Don't set your heart on property; don't worry about reputation in the world. Turn the other cheek. Make use of his directive not to respond to violence with violence. We are to be the children of the peaceable kingdom.

In his plan of salvation, Jesus made of no account the difference between rich and poor, saint and sinner. He called all alike to be his brothers and sisters, to be saved. He brought a cure for overly-moralistic religion by making baptism and Holy Communion, the sacraments of salvation, a gift. He overturned intellectual arrogance by making knowledge of salvation accessible only through faith. It is as available to the poor and unlearned as to the genius.

Jesus revealed that there is only one way to bring this Kingdom to which the Father has called us. "Thy kingdom come, thy will (Father) be done on earth as it is in heaven."

For only you, Father, created the kingdom and only you can bring it to maturity. You require that we cooperate by imitating Jesus in keeping the Commandments, following the way of the Gospel he lived and taught, and obeying his teaching Church.

In addition to these commands and guidelines of life we must add the most careful and prayerful attention to the personal inspiration the Holy Spirit gives us daily. Only with the Spirit's help can we serve the kingdom by all the prayers, works, joys and sufferings of each day, as we promise in the Daily Offering. The Spirit's inspiration has or will guide us in the choice of our state of life, our career choice, the friends and companions we choose, the goals we set for our lives. The Spirit guides us to repent of whatever wrong choices we have made. He directs us to be faithful to whatever binding commitments we have involved ourselves in. He will show us the way to holiness through our fidelity to our promises.

Jesus has appointed us to help bring the kingdom. Let there be no mistake about that.

He not only taught us to say, "Thy kingdom come"; he also said, "Take my yoke upon you," that is, "Work heart-to-heart with me to bring the kingdom." It's evident that he is saying of the kingdom, "You help to make it come."

Has not Jesus said, "Fear not little flock. The Father has been pleased to give you the kingdom"? The kingdom is ours and the responsibility for it is ours by baptism, by confirmation, and by the constant exhortation of the Church. When we're not part of the solution to the world's problems, we're part of the problem.

So many build their own private, selfish little kingdom with feverish activity. Yet God has called us to build only one kingdom, the kingdom of God.

In Europe during the Second World War, a statue of Christ was shattered. An artist was commissioned to restore it. When the restored statue was unveiled, the wrists were still shattered and the hands were missing. A placard announced, "You are the hands of

Christ." That is the truth. It accords with the test Jesus said we must pass at the Last Judgment: "I was hungry and you gave me food, I was thirsty and you gave me drink." God wants suffering overcome. He wants joy to prevail. Whoever does not help in the work will never enter the kingdom of God.

There are two ways of service in this kingdom. The first is to live as baptism requires, in whatever state of life one has chosen. A great help to it is to pray the Daily Offering of the Apostleship of Prayer, and live that offering by responding to the daily inspirations to serve Christ.

The second way is for those who, hearing his call in the Holy Spirit, have, in his own words, "given up house or brothers or sisters or mother or father or children or lands for my sake and for the sake of the Gospel." Jesus promises that they will "receive a hundred times more now in this present age... and eternal life in the age to come" (Mk 10:29-30).

This kingdom is spreading through time and space. It is *the* enterprise of creation. Unless our hearts join the Heart of Jesus in serving it earnestly, we are missing the full destiny to which Jesus invites us in the "Our Father." He once declared, "I have come to set the earth on fire" (Lk 12:49). Has his Heart set yours on fire? Have you come not just to know about him, but to know him, to become one of his close friends, loving and working with him personally, bringing the kingdom of God by cooperating with God's will in your life?

If you and I have caught that fire, then, when Christ has destroyed every power and principality and authority and restored the kingdom to God the Father, imagine our joy as we enter his Heart forever!

And let us not miss this point, that in inspiring us to pray for the coming of the kingdom, Jesus is teaching us to pray not just for the transformation of the world, but for his return to take us into the promised land, the house of the Father; and in doing it he is motivating us not to wait inactively but to work the harder to spread the Gospel by our own lives and service of love. In putting in our hearts and on our lips the petition, "Thy kingdom come," he is bringing forth from us the biblical "cry of the Spirit and the bride, 'Come, Lord Jesus!'" (Cf. CCC, ##2816-2818).

FIFTH DAY

PRAYING FOR OUR DAILY BREAD

"Give us this day our daily bread."
This petition came from Jesus' experience of the many hungers and thirsts of the human heart. Our novena goal is to enter the Heart of Jesus and the experiences, thoughts and feelings from which this petition came, and make them our own so we can pray and live the "Our Father" as Jesus did.

Where did the "Our Father" originate? Pilgrims to the Mount of Olives go to an unfinished Basilica of the Sacred Heart, which has a beautiful "Cloister of the Pater Noster," that commemorates what may be the place where Jesus taught his disciples the prayer. On the walls of the cloister and nearby structures, the "Our Father" is inscribed in 60 languages.

Each language and each heart interprets the prayer its own way, sometimes poorly. Let us unearth in this prayer for daily bread the very thoughts and feelings of the Heart of Jesus.

Jesus' compassion for the hungry fills the Gospels. His heartfelt concern led him to action. He fed the hungry. He urged upon all his followers for all time the duty of caring for the hungry.

But now we broaden our understanding of this petition. It came from Jesus' own human experience of the *many* hungers of the human heart: for food, for rest, for peace. Grieved by the many who rejected him, failed him, betrayed him, he experienced lifelong the human hunger for love.

He hungered for God the Father. In his Divine Nature, he was already with the Father; in his human nature he longed to ascend to him too! We are told how he used to go off to pray alone, and Luke tells us that on one occasion "He spent the night in prayer to God" (6:12).

The heart of Jesus, then, experienced our human hungers.

Surely Jesus is putting all of them into this petition to the Father. Someone might think, "You're exaggerating. The 'Our Father' says only, 'Give us this day our daily bread.'" But in fact, in Matthew, the Greek word can mean either "daily" or "future," or both. St. Jerome translated it, "supersubstantial," and then it surely refers to "the bread which comes down from heaven."

How could Jesus not have Holy Communion in mind here, when he said from the heart, "Do not work for food that perishes, but for the food that endures for eternal life, which the Son of Man will give you" (Jn 6:27). Let us not forget that the Church urges us to receive Holy Communion daily if we can, and that is what the Apostleship of Prayer tries to inspire us to do.

In the desert, Jesus was tempted by Satan to turn stones into bread, but we can think that even then he was planning to turn himself into bread, for as he said, "One does not live by bread alone" (Mt 4:4). At the Last Supper, when about to become himself the best Food of any meal ever eaten, he said, "I have eagerly desired to eat this Passover with you before I suffer" (Lk 22:15). That is language of the heart. He wants us too to speak from the heart to the Father when we ask for our daily bread, especially heaven's bread.

So we pray this prayer for bread. See how lovingly the Father answers us. He sends us his Shepherd-Son to lead us to his Church where we are fed on the bread of life. We can't thank him enough for Mother Church who feeds us with this bread; we can't pray enough for priestly vocations, and for faithful priests, and for faithful religious men and women who have formed so many of us in the faith and awakened our hunger for the bread of life. When Jesus was about to choose the first twelve Priest-Apostles he spent the night in prayer. His Heart is teaching us to have a like care for vocations. Imitate him!

How are we to receive this divine bread?

Joseph and Mary ate many ordinary human meals with Jesus. Those, too, were banquets of love. Surely, we can imitate them, and also Lazarus' sisters Martha and Mary. Recall how Jesus appreciated Mary's attentive, adoring love! But neither did he miss Martha's caring service. We must be like her in feeding his members, for "What you did for the least of these my brothers you did for me." Above all, we can ponder the Virgin Mary receiving Holy Communion from the Apostle John, and imitate her. She knows best how to return the love of the Heart of the God and Son who is our Food.

What, then does the Eucharistic Bread call us to do?

It calls us to return love for love. It calls us to love Christ's gift of himself so much that our love helps us throw off the chains of love for worldly things. We no longer cling desperately to health or wealth or honor or long life. He gave up all these things for us. We'll do it for him too.

The Eucharistic Bread inspires us to act as the Lord does. He feeds us on everything he has, even his own body and blood. We must help feed the hungers of others, above all by spreading the good news of the Gospel.

And so in praying for our daily bread, we pray for all peoples everywhere; and, as the Father's children, responsible with him for the kingdom, we work to see that the hungry are fed in his world. Our work and prayer always go together, for the feelings of a true heart are inseparable from the work of the hand, as with the human Heart and hands of Jesus.

We see that our Supersubstantial Bread calls us daily to the Mass to meet in wondrous mystery with Christ offering himself for us and giving himself to us. It supercharges us with the love we need to go out and serve the world according to his teaching, "I was hungry and you gave me to eat."

Think for a moment of the finest banquet you have ever shared. Are you sure the one you have thought of is the finest? Now, let me ask you: Did you think of Holy Communion? Surely our Lord would. Holy Communion is a banquet so divine that it will continue in Heaven, as the Council of Trent taught us in keeping with the Gospels. May we receive it daily until we receive it in the Eternal Day.

Let us close by praying the "Our Father" together, concentrating especially on the petition that we, the human race, have our hunger satisfied, especially the hunger for the Bread of Life come down from Heaven.

"Our Father...."

PRAYING TO BE FORGIVEN
AND TO FORGIVE

"Forgive us our trespasses as we forgive those who trespass against us." In this petition of the "Our Father," Jesus is
putting us on the road to eternal life, since forgiveness alone
opens the way closed by sin.

A traveler standing on the rim of the Grand Canyon gazes into
the distance, upon an unforgettable vista of towering iridescent
heights and dizzying depths stretching as far as the eye can see. Convert that vista into a spiritual one, in accord with the Invocation,
"Heart of Jesus, abyss of all virtues," and imagine our adoring won-
der at the vision before us.

We would see living love rising in all its transcendent heights,
and humility at its unmeasurable depths, and cascading from the one
to the other a great river of forgiveness.

We find ourselves appealing for that forgiveness in the petition
of the "Our Father" before us today: "Forgive us our trespasses as
we forgive those who trespass against us." Here, full force, is Jesus'
desire to have forgiveness fill all the hearts in the world.

Who hasn't experienced that isolated, anguished, guilty,
wrenching feeling of being cut off by sin, of needing to be forgiven
and put right with man and God? Mary Magdalene did; Peter did;
Judas did. Without forgiveness, hell would begin on earth; but the
forgiving Heart of Jesus makes this the land of beginning again.

The Gospels abound with Jesus' words and deeds of forgiveness. Over and over the Gospel uses one word to tell us what went
on in Jesus' Heart: *compassion.* Compassion is the virtue that makes
us hurt when another suffers, and moves us to action to relieve that
suffering. Jesus knew how people suffered when they needed forgiveness, and he gave it freely. He told parables of forgiveness. Who is

unmoved by his story of the Prodigal Son? He forgave the woman taken in adultery, and the Apostle Peter who denied him. As the nails were hammered into him he kept saying, "Father, forgive them, they know not what they do."

To inspire us to want, ask for, and practice forgiveness, it is helpful to look at the root of, the reasons for, and the results of forgiveness.

The root of forgiveness is love, not justice. If justice prevailed we'd all be condemned. Without forgiveness, there is no entrance into heaven.

God's unconditional fatherly love for all bulldozes away the boundaries between the righteous and the unrighteous by offering forgiveness and salvation to all, irrespective of merit. In his fatherly love he calls all of us who sin to amend. He gave us baptism and the blood of Jesus to offer in the Mass as the payment for our sins. This gives us all the more confidence in his fatherly forgiveness. But he does this only for those who do likewise by joining him in offering forgiveness to others.

The basic reason for forgiveness is that love always seeks reunion. The very reason Jesus came was to reconcile us to God and one another. But there are other reasons for forgiveness too, reasons so strong that we're commanded to forgive. It's urgent to note that in the "Our Father" we condemn ourselves if we're not forgiving, for we ask to be forgiven as we forgive!

Mutual forgiveness is necessary, because it is the only way to be God's united children. We repeatedly offend one another, so if we don't keep forgiving, love and unity will not last. That is why Jesus told Peter that we must forgive not seven times, but seventy times seven times.

Perhaps the case of Judas will give us still deeper insight. Jesus, even when he knew Judas was about to betray him, offered Judas the morsel of friendship at the Last Supper. But Judas remained stubborn in sin, and executed the betrayal. Then he despaired. Why, since he had seen how forgiving Jesus was?

There was a reason, and perhaps this is it: Only a person who loves deeply, deeply enough to be humble before the mystery of undeserved love, can see forgiveness as reasonable or believable. The proud and haughty cannot forgive those who injure their self-esteem or their reputation. And it seems they can't believe others can forgive either. If we are not forgiving, we are not likely to believe even in God's forgiveness. People to whom that happens cut themselves off from God's forgiveness, as Judas did.

We can learn another lesson from Judas' tragedy. It is that Jesus forgives sin and loves sinners, but never condones sin or accepts one who refuses to repent. And he calls us to imitate him. "If your right hand causes you to sin, cut it off and throw it away" (Mt 5:30). St. Augustine says somewhere that the right hand can be taken as referring to one's best friend.

Let us review what this petition calls us to do and resolve to do it.

It calls us to ask daily for forgiveness, for sins old and new, as we ask daily for bread. It insists that we in turn forgive by making us profess that we are forgiving. Jesus says expressly in the Gospel of Matthew, "If you do not forgive others, neither will your Father forgive your transgressions" (6:15).

This petition calls us to pay a debt of love to our forgiving Father, who gave us his forgiving Son and Holy Spirit, and wants a forgiving family. It invites us to beatitude, for it makes us peacemakers. One priest likes to say, "If you want to feel God's presence, forgive your enemy." This is in keeping with the beatitude, "Blessed are the peacemakers, for they will be called children of God" (Mt 5:9).

Is there anything more Christian, more Christlike, and more akin to the Heart of Jesus than forgiveness? It heals wounds, forgets the unforgettable, turns our enemies to friends, restores brotherhood, family and friendships, makes God's love visible in us, his images, attracts others to goodness, and stirs hope even among the most sinful.

May the Lord Jesus, when he looks into our hearts, see the depths of our lowliness, and see pouring from our love an ever-flowing cascade of forgiveness toward all. Then we can be assured that our forgiving hearts are united to the Heart of God's Son forever.

PRAYING TO WIN THE VICTORY

"Our Father who art in heaven.... Lead us not into temptation." As we continue our meditation on the source of the "Our Father" in the Heart of Jesus, we come to this perplexing, even unsettling, petition. It prompts in us the question: Does God really lead us into temptation?

The *Catechism of the Catholic Church* gives us the answer without wasted words: the phrase in the "Our Father" is a poor translation of a rich word in the original Greek language. It can better but less briefly be translated *do not allow us to enter or yield to temptation* (#2846).

Still, why didn't the Lord just have us say, "Keep us from having any temptation"? On reflection, we can see why. We know that if we're to lead a human life, we can't be saved from all trial. Life involves choices; where there are choices there are often temptations. Recall the story of the North Pole explorer who, when asked what he missed most up there, said, "Temptation."

Jesus himself "was led by the Spirit into the desert to be tempted by the devil." He had to face the issues as Adam and Eve did, and undo their sin by making the right choices. Jesus doesn't have us pray, "Keep us from any temptation," because we're his soldiers, and life is a warfare. Heaven is without temptation, not earth.

Babies must learn to walk even at the cost of bruises; mother birds must push their little ones from the nest to fly at last; Christians must fight evil at Christ's side. St. Teresa of Avila says good spiritual soldiers don't plead not to be sent into battle; they're eager to win the victory with Christ. What we do ask is not to be tempted beyond our strength, and not to have the devil deceive us by playing the role of an "angel of light."

St. James, perhaps fed up with nonsensical ideas, says clearly:

"No one experiencing temptation should say, 'I am being tempted by God'; for God is not subject to temptation to evil, and he himself tempts no one. Rather, each person is tempted when he is lured and enticed by his own desires" (Jm 1:13-14).

In his agony, Jesus prayed, "My Father, if it is possible, let this cup pass from me; yet, not as I will but as you will" (Mt 26:39). That is the spirit of this petition, a petition about which Jesus must feel strongly, for his Heart is "Victim for sin."

The Holy Spirit helps us discern between the trials of growth and the inducements to sin, so we can bear with the one and avoid the other. He unmasks the devil's lies to which Adam and Eve yielded. But our hearts will be open to the Spirit's guidance only if we pray and keep vigilant (CCC, #2847). We might summarize the meaning of this petition in the words, "Help us to be so faithful to you in our everyday prayers, works, joys and sufferings that we will be far from the weakness of will and dullness of heart that makes us fall into sin."

Like Jesus consoled by angels after his desert temptations, God rewards his faithful spiritual combatants by giving them a victory, a reward, and a bonus.

A victory: St. Paul says, "God is faithful and will not permit you to be tempted beyond your strength." He adds that God "will give you a way out that you may be able to bear it" (1 Cor 10:13).

God gives *a reward*. The Book of Revelation says: "He who overcomes, I will permit to sit on my throne with me" (Rv 3:21). He even gives *a bonus*, in which St. Paul delights where he writes, "Gladly will I glory in my infirmities that the power of Christ may dwell in me" (2 Cor 12:9-10).

Let me summarize and draw a conclusion.

To our petition, "Lead us not into temptation," the Father answers by setting up a roadblock to sin which could be put in these words: "I sent my Son to be Victim for your sins. See him being nailed to the cross in front of you. You can't take the road to sin without trampling him, and thrusting the lance of betrayal into his Heart. That's how I protect you from temptation."

Still, our sins and the sin and evil in the world do discourage us at times. Perhaps the Holy Father had that in mind when, meditating on the Invocation, "Heart of Jesus, in whom the Father was well pleased," he said, "Is not the Heart of Jesus then the 'point' in which the human person can regain full confidence in all that is created?" In other words, Jesus won the victory, and we can too. All we need do is get up one time more than we fall.

An A.A. member told this story: A cocky young demon landed on a Christian's shoulder and said, "You're discouraged." "No," came the reply, "I'm not." But with further probing, the man's shoulders slumped and he said, "Yeah, I'm discouraged," and yielded to temptation. The demon got a promotion, and was sent to tempt a more solid Christian. He jumped on the man's shoulder, went through his routine, and got nowhere. "I trust in the Lord," the Christian kept saying. "I take it day by day, hour by hour. If I fall I get up. The Lord always forgives." That night when Satan asked, "How did it go?" the demon's shoulders slumped. "I'm discouraged."

With the Lord on our side, who should be discouraged, Satan or us?

SEEKING THE GIFT OF ETERNITY

**"Our Father, who art in heaven... deliver us from evil."
Why does the perfect prayer end with a reference to evil instead of some glorious request to be called home to the glory
of the Trinity and the fulfillment of every desire of the human
heart? What does it mean to be fully delivered from evil?**

That question will help us continue our meditation on the "Our
Father" as a privileged way of learning more about the Heart of Jesus
from which the prayer came. This last petition can be a kind of let-
down. So my question prompts us to look more deeply into the wise
Heart of Jesus. What did he have in mind when he ended the "Our
Father" in this way?

Our hearts have felt the truth of the old saying, "Be it ever so
humble, there is no place like home." Why didn't Jesus close with
an expression of that longing in our hearts, "Bring us to your home
at last"?

Jesus shared the feelings those words express. During his time
on earth, his human Heart longed to go home to the Father, where
he had always been in his divine nature begotten of the Father, but
never in his human nature born of his Virgin Mother. Jesus expressed
that longing when he cried in ardor: "There is a baptism with which
I must be baptized, and how great is my anguish until it accomplished!" (Lk 12:50). He was speaking of the "baptism" of his death,
for only the outpouring of his Heart's blood would complete his work
of redeeming us, awaken the fire of our love, and open the way back
to the Father for him and for us.

When at last that hour was almost upon him he said, "In my
Father's house there are many dwelling places. If there were not
would I have told you that I am going to prepare a place for you?"
(Jn 14:2). Why did Jesus not end the "Our Father" with our plea to
go home?

Our task, then, is to enter his Heart with the help of the Gospels to learn why he chose instead to have us pray, "Deliver us from evil."

What does it mean to be delivered from evil? In the original Greek, the phrase can mean, "Deliver us from what is sick, in poor condition, painful, contagious, spoiled, worthless, base, bad, evil, wicked, vicious." It also means, "Deliver us from the Evil One." The *Catechism of the Catholic Church* says bluntly, "In this petition, evil is not an abstraction, but refers to a person, Satan, the Evil One, the angel who opposes God" (#2851).

What is evil but the opposite of good? What is good? Jesus said, "No one is good but God alone" (Lk 18:19). To be attached to anything but God is to be undelivered from evil. We won't be free of evil until we're free of Satan and all that tempts us from full allegiance to God.

Why, then, didn't Jesus just have us say, "Bring us home to you, God, the only Good"? The best answer may be his prayer to the Father at the Last Supper: "I do not ask you to take them out of the world, but to deliver them from the Evil One" (Jn 17:15).

Like Jesus, we can and should long to go home; but first, like him, we have the Father's work to do. So we're to ask God to guard us from overpowering temptations and to deliver us from evil, especially from the Evil One himself, while we complete our tasks. We must work on and live on until we can say with Jesus, as he said at the Last Supper, "I have glorified your name by accomplishing the work you gave me to do" (Jn 17:4).

What Jesus is teaching us to pray for is a final and full deliverance from Satan, sin and death. Implied in this petition is a prayer for our resurrection and eternal homecoming, for without these we can never be delivered from evil.

An important truth is coming to light here. It is that we can never understand a phrase like "deliver us from evil" except in the Heart of Jesus, through the Gospels. We must pray over the Gospels daily. It is there that we come to understand the Heart of Jesus and his teachings.

Jesus makes it evident in the Gospels that evil can't overcome us if we're faithful, for he has overcome the world, as he said at the Last Supper. He expects us to remember that he is our Resurrection and our Life, as he told Martha; he wants us to long for our quarters in his Father's house, which he went to prepare for us. He wants us to remember that "God is love," and let our hearts stir with longing to be with Love. How can we not long to see Love, and have Love and be loved by Love forever?

We need to pay special attention to the word *us* in the petition "Lead us not into temptation." We are praying "in communion with the whole Church, for the deliverance of the whole human family" (CCC #2850). Jesus does not allow us to be escapist, even in the name of going home to God. Like him we have to join prayer and action for our salvation and that of the whole world.

We can suppose, then, that in teaching us to pray to be delivered from evil, he expects us to realize we are praying to be with the good God even in this life. And to realize we must go on with our productive toil gladly for his sake until he calls.

This last petition can inspire us to redouble our efforts to redeem the time, pray daily, and carry out our tasks. That is the very program of the Apostleship of Prayer, the League of the Heart of Jesus. The Daily Offering is both a prayer and a promise to live what we offer in the prayer, for the whole world. If you don't belong to the Apostleship of Prayer, and pray and live the Daily Offering, I urge you to do so.

In the spirit of this last petition, then I pray, "Heart of Jesus, delight of all the Saints, lead us in the Holy Spirit to you, with Mary and the whole communion of Saints, to the Father's home, beyond all evil. Amen."

NINTH DAY

WHAT MARY KNEW ABOUT JESUS

The "Our Father" never mentions the Son of the Father, but by meditating on its petitions we have entered deep into the Son's Heart and learned more about him who is "meek and humble of heart," and we will go still deeper this last time.

In this last meditation we reflect on how the devotion to his human Heart helps us develop a more balanced understanding of his divine and human qualities. And then I will invite you to join the Apostleship of Prayer as a way to develop a more personal, heartfelt relationship and union with him through prayer and service.

The history of doctrine shows us that some Christians had a vice tangled in the folds of their faith. They "guarded" the doctrine of Jesus' divinity by claiming Jesus only appeared to have a body. They denied Mary was his real Mother. Their error was called the Gnostic heresy.

No Catholic holds that today, but some distance themselves from him by failing to realize how truly he was, and lived as, a human being. A woman came to a priest in search of relief from the cross she was carrying. His best assessment was that her burdens were the inescapable ones of her state of life, so he encouraged her to bear her cross as Jesus had borne his. She retorted, "Oh, but he was God!"

Wasn't that a failure to grasp how fully the Son of God lived a fully human life? The Letter to the Hebrews tells us he sympathizes with us because he "has similarly been tested in every way" we have, "yet without sin" (Heb 4:15).

Devotion to the Heart of Jesus helps us pay attention to his personal experiences as a human being. It helps us know for certain that Jesus, like us, had to bear his human burdens in a human way. Look in vain in the Gospels for a miracle he worked for his own convenience!

Devotion to his Heart is focused by some only on his feelings; but in both Scripture and contemporary usage, the phrase, "the heart of a man" refers to both affections and intelligence. By using Scripture to enter prayerfully into the mind and Heart of Jesus as God's word puts him before us during his lifetime on earth we can avoid sentimentality and practice devotion to his Heart in a balanced way. We also learn that like him we have to use all our human gifts in the service of Christ and the Father and of one another.

Our problem of knowing Jesus is opposite to that of Mary and his other contemporaries.

In his day, no one who knew him doubted he was a man. Mary could not doubt. She carried him nine months in her womb. She nursed him at her breast, tended his little hurts when he cried, fed him when he was hungry, raised him at her knee, and watched him grow to boyhood and manhood. She felt the weight of his blood-drenched dead body in her arms at the foot of the cross. She enjoyed the embrace of his risen body on the first Easter. And, thanks be to God, she shares what she knows with us when we pray her rosary.

His neighbors saw his rough hands and the rippling muscles of his trade, and demanded to know who he thought he was to presume to teach them — he, a carpenter, the son of Joseph, a carpenter!

Jesus's problem was not how to reveal his human nature, but how to reveal to them that he had a divine nature. He needed all his human graces and skills and more to solve it in human ways. Rejected by the leaders, his divinity unknown to his disciples, he went up Tabor and prayed for help. And there the Father gave him witness: "This is my beloved Son, with whom I am well pleased. Listen to him" (Mt 17:5).

Though there are some weak-faiths today, most of us born into the Faith have, since we were toddlers, come to know Jesus as the Son of God. We rightly cling to that — but sometimes so unthinkingly that we don't allow him a body and soul, mind and heart and free will as real and struggling as ours. That error deprives us of many benefits of the Incarnation.

It ignores the core of the mystery — that, being human, he had to live and struggle like us; had to use his human mind to make plans, and his human will to confirm them; and when they failed, change them, and go on. His divine powers he used to serve others, to manifest his divinity, and to help him carry out the Father's plan.

There are some rewarding and some demanding conclusions to all this for us.

First, there is the deeper entry into his mystery and a new closeness to him in the realization he is not only as human as you and I, he is more human. Sin dehumanizes. He never sinned. His human Heart beat and throbbed with the feelings, emotions, trials, temptations and tribulations we have. He was one of us.

Where does that leave us? With the realization that we have to live like him and for him. He needed the Father and needs us. The reason is not that he lacks power. It is because God the Father chose to save us by having him live a human life perfectly for us to imitate, and to leave the work of redemption in need of our contribution, for we too are his body.

"Take up my yoke upon you and learn of me, for I am meek and humble of heart." We learn about him, his yoke, and his Heart by sharing his prayers and his labors with him. That is our baptismal privilege and responsibility. A great help to being faithful is to say and live the Daily Offering.

Pope John Paul II said that the Apostleship of Prayer and its Daily Offering help Christians get hold of the fact that they "can be intimately united to Christ the Redeemer by offering their own life to the Heart of Christ." He praises the way the Apostleship draws us to center our lives on the Mass and the Eucharistic Heart of Jesus, and devote ourselves to the work of the kingdom; and the way it joins us to the Pope's monthly intentions for the needs and problems of the Church and the missions.[2]

The "Our Father" does not mention the Son. So his Church wrote the Daily Offering devoted to the Son and to union and solidarity with him in the work of redemption. The Church says the

---

[2] Address of Pope John Paul II to the Apostleship of Prayer, 4/13/85. Reprinted in *Prayer and Service*, Oct.-Dec. 1985, p. 259.

"Our Father" each day at Mass. We members of the Apostleship of Prayer say the Daily Offering each day to the Son, joining ourselves to him in his sacrificial offering in the Mass. I invite you to pick up the Daily Offering cards in the pews and say it with me now. Then I'll invite you to join the Apostleship of Prayer. All you need promise is to say and live the Daily Offering, and say at least one decade of Our Lady's rosary daily. I invite you to do this as a help to hold to and grow in what you have gained in this Novena.

Please join me:

"O Jesus, through the Immaculate Heart of Mary...."

I now invite you to pledge or renew membership in the Apostleship of Prayer. I will recite the pledge first so you may hear it, and then repeat it so you may say it with me.

Enrollment: (Plenary Indulgence)

LORD JESUS CHRIST—
I WISH TO BE A MEMBER—
OF THE APOSTLESHIP OF PRAYER—
I PROMISE TO SAY—
AND WITH YOUR HELP TO LIVE—
THE DAILY OFFERING.

I NOW ENROLL YOU OR RENEW YOUR ENROLLMENT IN THE APOSTLESHIP OF PRAYER, THE LEAGUE OF THE HEART OF JESUS, THE LEAGUE OF THE CIVILIZATION OF LOVE, THE KINGDOM OF THE HEART OF CHRIST.

Chapter Six

TO JESUS' HEART THROUGH THE *SEVEN LAST WORDS*

Homilies For
GOOD FRIDAY, FIRST FRIDAYS, RETREATS, AND HOLY HOURS

1. The First Word: *Father, forgive them*
2. The Second Word: *This day... with me in paradise*
3. The Third Word: *Behold your son....*
4. The Fourth Word: *I thirst.*
5. The Fifth Word: *My God, my God, why....*
6. The Sixth Word: *It is finished.*
7. The Seventh Word: *Father, into your hands....*

HOMILY ONE

THE FIRST WORD

"Father, forgive them, they know not what they do" (Lk 23:34).

HOMILETIC REALIZATIONS

A most gripping and salutary tradition of prayer is to spend, by meditation, Jesus' last hours with him on his deathbed, the cross, and meditate on his seven last words. But we have to know its value from our own prayerful experience, so that we can explain it in our homilies and draw people to practice meditation on Jesus' passion and death. And in the spirit of the Happy Death Society, we pray that Jesus will keep vigil with us at our deathbed, and lead us home to the Father.

A most powerful method of engaging in this prayer is to use our imagination as St. Ignatius of Loyola taught in his *Spiritual Exercises*. He wants us to go to Calvary in spirit to be with Jesus. We mobilize mind, heart, and imagination to join Mary. With her, we stand lovingly in the company of our Divine Friend in the pangs of his mortal hour. We are aware he has each of us pressed to his Heart even as he suffers.

Pius XII assured us of this. His encyclical *On the Mystical Body of Christ* tells us that Jesus, during his life on earth, knew and loved each of us personally and unceasingly (#75). Meditation on Jesus's seven last words is a way of telling the Savior that his disciple in turn is with him in his hour of need.

All through meditation on Calvary we should keep in mind what Jesus is doing there: dying for our sins. And doing it even as his jeering observers mock him because he saved others but can't save himself.

Is there any truth in their charge that he can't save himself? A

Catholic chaplain in the Korean war told how, at one point, a squadron of American soldiers was given the command, "Stand and die!" For them there was no hope of victory, and no retreat. They must delay the advance of the enemy so that the rest of the army might be saved. They did as commanded. By the time they were overrun, the rest of the army had withdrawn and regrouped and were saved.

Jesus, too, in the Garden the night before he died, had received from his Father the command, "Stand and die." In Jesus' case, we are the rest of the army. But we can see it is unthinkable that the Father approved of evil doers unjustly tormenting and killing his innocent Only Son. So we have to look further to come to some understanding of what is going on.

The fourth century Father of the Church, St. Gregory Nazianzen, gives us help. He called it inconceivable that the Father wanted the gory death of his Only Son as a ransom paid to him for our salvation.[1] What is the answer, then? In this matter as in many others, we need to distinguish between God's will of good pleasure and his permissive will. Just as there are many things we allow to happen though we disapprove of them, there are many more things the all-powerful Father is displeased with, but permits so that in the end all things may work together for our good. The Father certainly did not want Jesus to be killed unjustly, but neither did he want Jesus to abandon his post. If the Father did not ask Jesus to stand firm, would we be ready to accept when he asked a similar thing of us? In some deep and mysterious sense, the death of Jesus was necessary for our salvation, "since we are now justified by his blood" (Rm 5:9).

There is another truth at work in his jeerers' conviction that Jesus could not save himself. Love for us overcame Jesus' power to abandon us and save himself. Is it not a paradox that the possession most worthy of pride is love, yet the last thing a lover can be is proud, because he is helplessly dependent on the free gift of love returned by the beloved. So Jesus died because the crucifixion was required by the Father and by our need.

---

[1] See J.N.D. Kelly, *Early Christian Doctrines*, pp. 383-4.

What we learn and gain standing with Mary as Jesus dies is beyond telling, but a few things can be said.

A person opens his heart at two times above all others. The first time is in prayer, for God knows everything anyway. The second is on his deathbed, because it is his last chance to do so. On Calvary, where Jesus is both in prayer and on his deathbed, he opens his Heart through his words and through the wound in his side. Here is fulfilled his promise, "Let anyone who thirsts come to me and drink. Whoever believes in me, as Scripture says: Rivers of living water will flow from within him" (Jn 7:38).

By being present, through prayer, on Calvary, at the one and only time the Holy Sacrifice is offered in blood outpoured, we learn to offer the same Sacrifice in the unbloody manner of the Mass.

We must also learn there how to imitate Jesus when the time comes for us to hang on the Calvary of our lives, as it will. Suffering, above all unjust suffering such as Jesus endured, can shake us loose from our deepest commitments, whether to marriage, parenthood, priesthood, religious life or simply responsible work for our livelihood. When suffering comes many walk away from faith and faithfulness. The lesson, then, of how to bear suffering, is a lesson of salvation.

Padre Pio, the stigmatic whose wounds would bleed even when he was offering Mass, once said, "The person who is sick is offering Mass."[2] It is on Calvary where the Mass in blood was first offered that we learn to offer the Mass in the daily sufferings of our lives. It is on Calvary that we learn the meaning of the Daily Offering in which we join everything to the Heart of Jesus and his Holy Sacrifice every day for the salvation of all.

Followers who spend time often with Jesus on Calvary will never abandon Jesus when they hang on their own Calvary. They will even learn to make his seven last words their own. The *Catechism of the Catholic Church* says that Jesus gives us a glimpse into his bottomless filial prayer "in *his last words* on the cross, where prayer and

---

[2] *A Padre Pio Profile* by John A. Schug, p. 62.

the gift of self are but one (#2605)." On Calvary, we can learn from Jesus the secret of how to live out in our daily lives the promise we make in prayer of giving self to God and one another.

When we preach on the seven last words, we need to provide people with reflections such as these to help them better appreciate the function of meditation on the passion. It is one of the most powerful ways of learning that the Son of God "has loved me and given himself up for me" (Gal 2:20).

The First Word

FATHER FORGIVE THEM

We will be blessed if in the course of our lifetime we learn the full extent of this forgiving act of Jesus, apply it to ourselves, and imitate it. We have to learn that his words of forgiveness ring through all times and all places.

The experience of a little boy can help to bring out what is really happening on Calvary. The boy was taken to visit his maternal grandfather on his deathbed. The loving old man gave the child his gold watch. In no time the boy dropped it and broke it and felt very bad about it.[3] The eternal Father gave the human race the gift of his own Son. What have we done with that gift? His final scream will rent the air in answer and tell us how much he had to forgive us: all the sins of all of us of all time.

"Father, forgive them, they know not what they do" (Lk 23:34). By entering into this moment of Jesus' passion, we have a chance beyond compare of learning how forgiving the human heart can be, and of how forgiving Jesus wants our hearts to be.

In spirit, we arrive at Calvary with Jesus, amid friend and foe. "They gave him wine drugged with myrrh, but he did not take it" (Mk 15:24). He chooses to stay alert through all the suffering to come, atoning for those who abuse their lives with drugs to escape life's pain. He gives example to people tempted to abandon their duties and charges when pain and trouble come. He is saying no to suicide when life begins to flicker and burdens to mount. He has learned from the Father that the work of life is to love and to pray and to serve. He will love on and pray and serve to the end.

Soldiers begin pulling off his clothes, and tearing off his skin

---

[3]   This is a memory from the author's own childhood.

with them because the blood of the scourging has dried. Throwing him down upon the cross they begin nailing him, the beat of the hammer accenting the cries of rejection and mockery from those he loves.

Such uncompensated suffering is the most unendurable. To endure it he first underwent his final lesson in obedience in his agony in the Garden where he accepted the Father's will.

The terrible pain begins. Executioners drive the heavy spike through the complex of nerves and bone of the foot. Have you ever, when sharp pain struck, cried out and cursed? The ancient philosopher Seneca wrote that so great was the pain of crucified men that they cursed their birth, their mothers, and their executioners. The ancient statesman Cicero adds that they so blasphemed the gods a new indignity was inflicted on them. Their tongues were cut out.

Watching friends and foes knew these things, and knew he had told his followers to love their enemies and do good to those who hate them. They waited to see how these fine teachings would be lived by him in his screaming pain. He had said that the mouth speaks from the fullness of the heart. They awaited his word according to the heart of each, from the torn Heart of the Virgin to the gloating heart of the grossest one there. What is in our hearts as we wait?

"Father," he cries, "Father, forgive them." His answer was not a curse but a prayer. He who had said, "Pray always," prayed for his crucifiers. Not only did he cry it; the Greek text indicates he kept crying it. Forgive them. Forgive them.

We who love him have here proof for our trust in his love. Torture, betrayal, hatred cannot change that loving Heart in that breast torn by sorrow and pain. "Love is as strong as death," it was written. He is proving it stronger.

He went beyond forgiveness. He reached for a shred of excuse for them. "They know not what they do." They know not what they do, they know not what they do. "They" don't know. Who are "they"? Do we know full well that "they" are *us*? Christ died for us, for our sins.

The *Catechism of the Catholic Church* says that, "Taking into account that our sins affect Christ himself, the Church does not hesitate to impute to Christians the gravest responsibility for the torments inflicted upon Jesus, a responsibility with which they have all too often burdened the Jews alone." It explains that the reason is because "sinners were the authors and the ministers of all the suffering that the divine Redeemer endured," and that our crime is greater because we know this and sin anyhow (#598).

If Christ died for our sins, yet we go on sinning, what are we doing? If we refuse any responsibility for Christ's death, are we not denying that our sins required his death if we are to be saved? Are we not rejecting his salvation?

St. Paul refers to our part in the death of Christ when he condemns unworthy Holy Communion. "Whoever eats the bread or drinks the cup of the Lord unworthily will have to answer for the body and blood of the Lord... and drinks a judgment on himself" (1 Cor 11:27, 29).

Hearing Jesus forgive, we learn to trust his love, and to imitate it. We trust him with all our sins. We hide nothing from the Church and the confessional. We wash ourselves there in his copious blood outpoured. With love and devotion, we renounce all sin.

Once we learn these things it is our turn to live them. Forgiveness begins at home. We must not be like Hitler, who first "warred" with his father, then went out and went to war with the world. Out of love for and likeness to Jesus we mend our quarrels. Scripture tells us to settle before sundown.

But we have to go beyond forgiving our enemies to loving them, as Jesus did and taught.

Abraham Lincoln once set a fine example of this. During the Civil War, he was asked by a southern mother to free her captured son to work on her farm to save her from hunger. He did as she asked. A northern woman, hearing of this, stormed up to him and said, "You don't free your enemy. You destroy him!" He replied, "Madam, if I make my enemy my friend, don't I destroy my enemy?"

Isn't this what we too are to do? Didn't Jesus come into a world at enmity with God, and is he not still at work to make friends of all, including you and me? So let us imitate our divine Lord by saying, *Father, forgive them; forgive all who offend you; forgive all who offend me. And forgive me as I want to be forgiving. Amen.*

THIS DAY... WITH ME IN PARADISE

The second word of Jesus invites us to reflect on how a thief became good, how this illumines for us the mystery of suffering, and how we must imitate Jesus in that mystery.

How a thief became good is a lesson we all need to learn to escape sin, because all sin is thievery of what does not belong to us.

So let us recollect ourselves, and become present to the mystery of Calvary. We hear passing travelers bad-mouthing Jesus along with his condemned companions. We hear them saying, *Look at those law-breakers. Good riddance!*

In our own day, one policeman tells how he used to call broken people "animals." Then he learned of a young man who became a "good thief." Formerly, he had been a car thief. Once, he even tried unsuccessfully to run over an officer who attempted to arrest him. Years later, the young man became a priest. Some who knew his record were hostile, but the policeman befriended and encouraged him. "You're a good priest," he said.

Recall that, at the Last Supper, Jesus foretold how, as the Scriptures had prophesied, he would be "counted among the wicked" (Lk 22:37). Now it is happening, and we even hear one of the criminals crucified with Jesus joining in the abuse. "Aren't you the Messiah? Then save yourself and us" (Lk 23:39).

The other criminal crucified with him, whom we have come to call the Good Thief, has been observing and listening to everything, as criminals do to survive. He knew a little about Jesus, as did most in Jerusalem. He may have remembered hearing that Jesus was criticized for eating with sinners. He didn't know that Jesus fed sinners on his own body and blood at the Last Supper. He was astounded by the first word of Jesus. He himself had probably done his share of cursing and screaming when he was nailed. He marvels at how any-body suffering so much can be so forgiving, so free of hate. Perhaps he really is the Messiah! Looking down at the Mother of Jesus, the criminal feels any remaining doubts tottering when he sees on Mary's face the grief, sorrow and compassion for her innocent lamb being slaughtered before her eyes. And we, seeing what is happening to this sinner, can we not see Mary's hand at work in his behalf?

Beginning to believe now, he comes to the point that he can't stand his fellow criminal's mocking of Jesus, and tells him to shut up. "Have you no fear of God?" he demands. By contrasting him-self with the good Jesus, he sees and confesses his own sinfulness. "We have been condemned justly," he cries to the mocker. "But this man has done nothing wrong." Then he who had marveled at Jesus praying himself prays despite his torment. "Jesus, remember me when you come into your kingdom."

The Good Shepherd's answer to his prayer goes beyond the request, to virtual canonization. For, though his feet are nailed, and he cannot walk in search of the lost, and though his arms are nailed and he cannot reach out to embrace them, his heart is free and goes out still. "Amen, I say to you," he calls out, "this day you will be with me in paradise" (Lk 23:39-43). And so the Good Shepherd teaches us that even for one on his deathbed it is not too late to cry to the Good Shepherd for salvation. Never despair of anyone. Perhaps even the parents of this Good Thief had written him off, and yet he would be in Heaven before them.

The Good Thief and the whole complex situation pro-vokes many thoughts about the mystery of suffering.

How many of us would have recognized Christ in a naked, tor-tured "criminal"? If, when suffering comes, it tempts us to doubts of faith, how could we have the faith to see God's Son in the Third Sufferer on Calvary? And how many of us when we suffer have said like the Good Thief, "I deserve it"?

When we find suffering turning us in on ourselves to the for-getfulness of others, do we recall how Jesus fought off that tempta-tion and imitate him? He heard the piteous bleating of the lost sheep and his heart went out to him.

Attention to the noble way Jesus suffered is what drew the heart of the Good Thief to Jesus and to repentance. Meditation on the passion of Jesus can do the same for us. Jesus himself foretold it: "When I am lifted up from the earth," he said, "I will draw everyone to myself" (Jn 12:32).

Calvary is a cure for impatience. Impatience is unwillingness to suffer. It is shameful, and it is wrong. "Whoever wishes to come after me," Jesus said, "must deny himself, take up his cross, and follow me" (Mk 8:34).

One priest said to his mother in illness: "I'm praying God to take away your sufferings, but if not, to put you with Jesus hanging on the cross, so none of your sufferings will be wasted. They will help in your own redemption and your children's and the world's." That is the grace we should all pray for in suffering.

The saints find joy in suffering. If we ask how, the answer is that happiness is not the lack of suffering. It is the presence of God.

Why do we understand suffering so little except that we refuse to meditate on the evil of sin? Either God is unjust, or sin is so terrible that the All-Merciful lets us suffer for correction and reparation and atonement with Jesus. The Good Thief understood: He deserved it; Christ did not!

There are three types of sufferers: The unrepentant waste their suffering; the repentant accept their due; the loving make atonement for their sins and the sins of others in union with Jesus. The writer Frank Sheed said that "The mystery of suffering is not that there is so much of it but that so much of it is wasted."

The great grace of the Good Thief is that he had the honor of being Christ's companion on Calvary, suffering with him for the redemption of the world. We should be happy for him and wish we had his chance, and realize that in a sense each of us does, as St. Paul realized: "I rejoice in my sufferings for your sake," he wrote to the Colossians, for "in my flesh I am filling up what is lacking in the afflictions of Christ on behalf of his body, which is the Church" (1:24).

It's time to formulate certain guidelines to take into life from this second word of Jesus on the cross. The first concerns our attitude toward capital punishment. The second concerns our attitude toward personal suffering.

The brutal infliction of capital punishment on our own innocent Savior has led the Church to abhor capital punishment, and the conversion of the Good Thief has made us the more mindful of the need to give wrongdoers the chance to reform. Pope John Paul II has recently taught that the traditional teaching of the Church "does not exclude recourse to the death penalty, if this is the only possible way of effectively defending human lives against the unjust aggressor," but that today "the cases in which the execution of the offender is an absolute necessity are very rare, if not practically nonexistent" (*Evangelium Vitae*, #56).[4] This, then, is one truly Christian guideline to form our attitude and our conscience in social and political life.

The second guideline concerns our attitude toward personal suffering. The truth is that in our sufferings we, like the Good Thief, can hang with Jesus in spirit and with him work the redemption; that no suffering, then, need be wasted; that we will not escape suffering because we carry its causes in our own person and meet them in the world around us; and that the choice that lies before us is to bear them like the Good Thief or like the unrepentant one. So let us resolve to make our suffering what it is meant to be by God, a share in the redemptive work of Jesus and his body the Church. Let us say to him "These wounds my Lord, thou makest thine / Share them with me for they are mine."

---

[4] See also *Catechism of the Catholic Church*, #2226, 1267, revised text.

BEHOLD YOUR SON.
BEHOLD YOUR MOTHER.

St. Paul, persecutor of Christ, renounced his blindness and became so fully a Christian he learned to say, "I live, yet no longer I, but Christ lives in me" (Gal 2:20). Marvelous though that is, he was only reflecting what Jesus promised all of us: "Whoever eats my flesh and drinks my blood remains in me and I in him" (Jn 6:56).

In that spirit of mystical union with him, we enter and identify with our dying Jesus and his experience.

We look down through his eyes, through his bleary vision, and share the feelings arising from what is seen. Swimming below is the oval face of Mother Mary. Its surface, a crystal lake reflecting a stormy sky above, mirrors every wound she sees, every unseen suffering, even the inmost agony, for heart is joined to heart.

He sees that care-worn face, no longer young. She who has never spared herself in caring for him and for so many others now needs care and support herself. To whom entrust her? To whom give her—for give her he must. Before closing his eyes in death, he must give everything away.

Beside her floats the bearded face of John, a truly faithful apostle—a stunned face, like a stricken animal dying, losing all as he sees Life dying. He needs support, lest he fall away in the darkness. What is to be done for them, for her and for him?

Jesus turns his eyes to his Mother. Her eyes meet his as no others can. His lips open to words eternally fated: "Behold your Son." *Behold your Son, dying on the cross, and being born at your side in John, as I will be born in all times and all places throughout history. Woman, new Eve, lover of all who live, behold your Son as you keep giving birth to the one you bore in Bethlehem.*

His eyes turn to John, John's to his. "Behold your mother."

Behold your Mother in your new life, your life in me, sharing my life, sharing my person, the person of the Son of God and the Son of Mary. My mother is your mother, for my life is your life.

You can understand, little one, only if you recognize the Last Adam before you and the New Eve at your side. The Last Adam is falling asleep. You will then see flowing from his side the living water I promised beforehand, the river that will regenerate the world, through baptism and Eucharist—the rivers that are "being" and "life" for the New Eve and for all her children. The New Eve at your side must complete her motherhood in you and in all the members of my body, the Church.

Now you and I need to hear Jesus speaking these same mysteries to us. We need to ponder their meaning, a meaning as real as our birth from our earthly mother.

We can understand only if we look at Jesus and Mary on Calvary and see the Last Adam and the New Eve before us. The Fathers of the Church and the scriptural exegetes point out that St. John in his Gospel brings out the parallel between what happened in the Garden of Eden and what happened on Calvary.

The stripping of garments is the return to the naked innocence of Eden. The pierced side of Adam foretold the pierced side of Jesus, and the new Eve coming forth in the rivers of living water is the Church, the bride of Christ and mother of all the living. Mary, conceived immaculate by the foreseen merits of Christ on the cross, was given birth beforehand to be the member of the Church who is also Mother of the Church.

Ezekiel foresaw the living waters, the wonder-stream, flowing from the side of the Temple (47:1-12). He saw the waters begin as a trickle, a wonder-stream that swelled as the waters flowed, until they became a river one could cross only by swimming. That wonder-river from the pierced side of the living Temple on the cross has become so great that it has baptized a billion living souls in our own time.

To try to condense and summarize these revelations that are as deep and mysterious as the wonder-stream, we need Mary's help.

What were her thoughts as she heard this third word, addressed to her and to each of us, her child? In Brazil a mother lost her teenage son to a young murderer. She went to his cell and said, "Last night you killed my son. Now you must take his place." She visited him for years, and then he said, "I was nothing but an animal before that woman came into my life; she's made me into a human being." Has not Mary done that times without number?

Our Lady's motherhood of each of us is even more loving and more profound. She gives birth to and receives each of us not as a substitute for Jesus but as his fullness, one day to bear all his gracious and noble qualities. This is not figurative language. She is our Mother. In the order of the supernatural life we are alive by the life of her Son. Since life is what every mother gives her child, Mary, the New Eve, is our Mother and the Mother of all the living.

She was immaculately conceived by anticipation, but she too is alive from the graces that flow from her Son, the graces he won on the cross. She is continuing to become the Mother of his full body, the Church, of which she is both Mother and member.

We need to take these truths to heart and live them, as did John. We are told that "From that hour the disciple took her into his home" (Jn 19:28). We know we are in Mary's care. But have we taken Mary into our care? John did. Not only did he need her; she needed him. He would be her support. And she needs us.

Imagine the devotion with which she participated in the Holy Sacrifice of the Mass as John offered it through the years. Imagine her receiving Holy Communion from his hand. Can any of us participate in the Mass with due devotion unless we stand often at the foot of the cross with Mary?

Let us not try to elude the fact: Mary is in our care. Her reputation is in our hands in our times. It is dependent on our loving and honoring her, spreading her devotion, and above all, doing her deeds of love, sinless, and obedient, living as she lived, being truly her children.

This is a duty to take seriously. We help fulfill her prophecy, "All generations will call me blessed." She wants us to attract her children to her. As she looks down on all her children, can't we hear her say to us as her Son did, "What you do unto others you do to me"? She says to each of us, *I am in need as I was in need when John cared for me. Today my name must be honored that people may be drawn to my Son. My children must be cared for that my Son's love and my love may shine forth in the world and draw all to salvation.*

In this age of longevity, this serving and honoring of Mary must be especially evident in the way we take care of our parents, and show care for other aged persons who come into our lives. The dying Jesus has put Mary and her children into our care. We are not mere infants given into her care, but, like John, adults caring for her as well. Are we fulfilling our responsibilities—bringing consolation to the heart of Jesus as he, hanging upon the cross, foresees our lives in him? Let us then, turn to Mary, and say, "Mary, my Mother, I will take you into my care."

The Fourth Word

I THIRST

"I thirst!" We can only feel and grapple with the intensity of the agony propelling this cry of Jesus from the cross if we forget our identity and enter into his.
Thirst was nothing new to Jesus. The Holy Land, apart from such lovely regions as its fruitful plain of Sharon, its Jordan Valley and Jericho with its waving palms, and the rolling forest glades of northern Galilee, is mostly a parched and thirsty land. Water is life, and water is rare.

The night before this torment on Calvary, Jesus in his agony poured out a bloody sweat. This morning his life's blood flowed out of a hundred wounds of scourging and seeped into the crown of thorns as well. It sprang out of the gaping wounds of hands and feet to dye crimson the spikes of crucifixion. We know of no one who offered him a drink to quench his thirst since the Last Supper, except for the drugged wine that he refused.

As his members, one in life with him, we enter in to share his state and feel his thirst and think his thoughts. If I may presume to turn his feelings and sensations into words, they might sound like this: *My body is one bleeding wound parching me to the heart. I fulfill my Psalmist's prophecy: "My throat is dried up like baked clay, my tongue cleaves to my jaws" (Ps 22:16). Why did my Psalmist not add that my heart is more parched than my cracked tongue—for I look out on a sea of unloving faces, indifferent faces, hostile, rejecting faces. My prophet Jeremiah foretold my heart's anguish when he wrote the words, "My breast! My breast! How I suffer! The walls of my heart!" (4:19). My Heart has to find a vent! I must open my mouth and cry out!*

And so all of us present on Calvary, friend and foe, hear his fourth word, that tormented cry: "I thirst!" It is a cry calling all people of all time until the end of time to respond by coming to quench his thirst.

How many have understood the true range of that thirst? Let us try to understand by entering first into his bodily sufferings, and then his mental and emotional sufferings.

Who present that day could have doubted his bodily sufferings? Like Mary, they saw that bleeding body hanging in agony, that body she knew since she conceived him and gave him birth.

How could anyone of any time doubt his bodily sufferings? Strangely, some have. The Gnostic heretics did. They could not believe God's Son took a real body. Sordid human flesh was far below his dignity! It was only an apparent body, they thought, that hung on the cross.

Some unthinking Catholics seem to fare little better. When told to bear their sufferings as Jesus did, they are inclined to say, "Oh, but he was God!" As if that made his sufferings go away! Do you think his Mother, Mary, who knew that body since conception and birth, could say such a thoughtless thing? Or Joseph, who many times must have warded off from him the little pains and hurts of childhood? In the great summary of the mystery of our faith, Jesus is everything that God is, and everything that we are, except sin. Having a more sensitive soul than any sinner, Jesus suffered more than all others in both body and soul. "Since the children share in flesh and blood," says the Letter to the Hebrews, "he likewise shared in them... tested through what he suffered" (Heb 2:14, 18).

Unbearable as Jesus' physical sufferings were, his mental and emotional sufferings dwarf them. The deepest thirst of us all is for love. He was parched for the love he is being refused throughout history. It has been shown that babies deprived of love and fondling pine away and die. Jesus' Heart, bursting with rejected love, has a Sahara of thirst for love.

Jesus needs love and wants love. What is he doing about it? Dying. Suffering is in the world, said Pope John Paul II in *Salvifici Doloris*, to unleash love. Jesus said it before him, about his own suffering: "When I am lifted up from the earth, I will draw everyone to myself" (Jn 12:32).

People today think it below their dignity to ask for compassion even from God. They have lost their way. In *Dives in Misericordia*, the Pope says of Jesus that when he is nailed to the cross, "The one who 'went about doing good and healing' and 'curing every sickness and disease' now seems himself to merit the greatest mercy and to *appeal for mercy*" (#68). Did not the Good Thief show Jesus mercy, since asking salvation of Jesus was like saying "I won't let your goodness and love go to waste. Please use it to save me."

In crying "I thirst!", Jesus is clamoring to us: "Don't waste your hearts! Use them to love the God who made you and is dying to save you!"

When he bows his head in death and allows his side to be pierced, his Heart will release into the world "rivers of living water," the waters of the Holy Spirit of Love. Then none who will to love will fail to love if they come to him and drink.

Mother Teresa of Calcutta once said of his cry of thirst, "It was a thirst for your love and my love and our love for one another." This is the power of freedom that God has given us. We can withhold love even from him. It is that from which he is dying. According to one medical analysis of the water and the blood already separated when they flowed from his pierced Heart, Jesus died of a broken Heart.

Let us ponder then our lifelong response to his cry, "I thirst!"

The sin in our every sin is our failure to love. But sin can be overcome. "I may have sinned gravely," said St. Bernard, "but what sin is there so deadly that it cannot be pardoned by the death of Christ?" The Good Thief made the point convincingly before him.

Jesus came to inflame love. "I have come to set the earth on fire, and how I wish it were already blazing!" (Lk 12:49). Will he refuse it to any who want to be inflamed? Will we do our part to set the fire, at least in ourselves?

Jesus is not crying out for himself alone, but for all in all history who are thirsty for love and life and all its good things. The

Catechism of the Catholic Church says of the cry of Jesus following his seven last words: "All the troubles of all time, of humanity enslaved by sin and death, all the petitions and intercessions of salvation history are summed up in this cry of the incarnate Word. Here the Father accepts them and, beyond all hope, answers them by raising his Son. Thus is fulfilled and brought to completion the drama of prayer in the economy of creation and salvation" (#2606).

Jesus still hungers and thirsts in others, and says to us, "What you do to others you do to me." He hungers and thirsts for good, holy, chaste companions. He thirsts until we renounce sin and become his faithful companions.

Father, I look on the loving, thirsting Jesus, to be freed of the selfishness which binds my love. Send the Holy Spirit of Jesus to grieve in me, grieve in atonement for all the sins that caused Jesus to thirst for love, grieve for all who need to be loved and all who do not love. Let your spirit of devotion well up in us, giving us the readiness to do your holy will as Jesus did. Father, the Divine Bridegroom of our souls cries to us, "I thirst!" Pour into us the love we need to give him to drink. Help us to quench his thirst. Amen.

The Fifth Word

MY GOD, MY GOD,
WHY HAVE YOU FORSAKEN ME?

Is not the fifth word from the cross the most God-forsaken cry in history? We must penetrate and grapple with the meaning of this terrible cry, heard before from many lips throughout history, but shocking to hear fly from the lips of the Nazarene.

Why so shocking on his lips? Because he is the God-Man, the Holy One of Israel. He is the Son of God in human nature, body and soul, crying out his feelings of dereliction to the Father and the Holy Spirit and to his own divinity. It is, as it were, the cry of God abandoned by God.

Let us enter deeper into that psychic darkness. Jesus was crucified about nine in the morning. By noon, darkness had fallen on the land. From the Gospel accounts, it seems that during the following three hours of darkness, silence and suffering were unrelieved by a word of his. Then he shattered the air and the silence with the frightful cry: "My God, my God, why have you forsaken me?" (Mt 27:46).

Can we delve into the depths of this unsettling mystery? Someone might say reassuringly, "Don't be upset. Any Jew hearing those words of the Jewish Jesus would recognize he is quoting the first words of Psalm 22, as a dying Christians might say those of the 'Our Father.' Psalm 22 begins alarmingly, but ends in victory."

Unfortunately, that reassurance is shrunken if not shattered by the fact that Psalm 22 is an alarming *prophecy* of the passion of the Messiah, a prophecy of his darkness, his torn heart, his sayings, doings and feelings—so we're back to the darkness! We also have to attend to the fact that Jesus cried out with the loud voice of a man in agony, not a teacher presenting doctrine.

Let us ponder and dig deeper into this deep mystery of faith, aware that by a mystery of faith we don't mean we can understand nothing, but only that we cannot understand everything.

At the Last Supper Jesus said, "Behold, the hour is coming when each of you will be scattered to his own home and you will leave me alone. But I am not alone because the Father is with me" (Jn 16:32). Beside this teaching of Jesus about the Father's presence, the Church teaches that Christ in his humanity had a direct knowledge and awareness of his divinity. This one Person we're talking about is both divine and human, God and Man. How then this terrible experience? What are we dealing with?

We are dealing with three hours of torment laced with unimaginable suffering and silence. What was Jesus doing during those three hours? What was he even capable of doing? This much we can say: He was dying and he was probably praying and wrestling with submission to his torment. His praying and his dying can help us grasp something of the mystery.

Jesus prayed all his life. This is his most terrible prayer, one of utter desolation and dereliction. To understand better, we enter into his Heart. We must not be afraid we are violating a sanctuary too sacred for us. It is our right. St. John Eudes reminds us we are his body, and adds, "He belongs to you as the head belongs to the body. All that is his is yours: breath, heart, body, soul and all his faculties. All of these you must use as if they belonged to you, so that in serving him you may give him praise, love and glory."[5] So we dig deeply into this mystery.

Jesus, we enter your Sacred Heart and try to sense the answer to our questions: Did you feel abandoned? You are human like us. You had human feelings. *How could you feel otherwise?* Even when we know we're not abandoned, but don't understand what is going on, we can feel abandoned like a frightened child. Yes, you felt abandoned, as your words make plain, and Mary felt abandoned with you,

---

[5]　*The Divine Office*, August 19, Feast of St. John Eudes.

as did Mary Magdalene and John and the apostles who felt so abandoned they ran away.

Did you think you were abandoned? Here we are drowning in mystery too deep for us, but let us bravely push on. We are really dealing with three questions, the first of which we have answered: Did you feel abandoned? Did you think you were abandoned? Were you abandoned?

Did you think you were abandoned? We have entered into your Heart and mind. It is almost three o'clock, the fatal hour. You are dying. We have seen dying people. The brain ceases to function properly. There may be drifting off into delirium. Your human brain is not exempt from the laws of biology. We feel the rising waters of death drowning out life and thought. Death is only minutes away. We feel you dying. Thought is clouded, for your human nature is our human nature. Whatever your mysterious human awareness and sight of God through your human intelligence operating by your bodily brain, it would cease as your brain died and you lost your mental powers. Perhaps in this moment you lost all conscious contact with God in experience or reason. Who then knows the answer to our question? Was your darkening consciousness so totally absorbed in the process of dying that you no longer knew you were not abandoned? Only God knows. Jesus, I think you may have had in a more terrible way the experience of many a sinner and many a mystic.

Were you abandoned? Some people in your shoes would consider themselves abandoned. The Father didn't work miracles to free you from the ordeal of dying. Many who ask God to free them from suffering feel they are abandoned if he doesn't. But they're not, any more than you were, Jesus. It is our faith: You are God. You cannot abandon yourself.

In any true sense, Jesus was not abandoned. No one who accepts God is ever abandoned by God: "I will espouse you to me forever," God has assured his people (Hosea 2:21). Whatever doubts those at the foot of the cross had when they heard those terrible words, the doubts were swept away when they saw Jesus risen from the dead.

We must learn from this experience of Jesus not to panic in our own dark hours.

We are staring into the depths of the mystery of our faith. If we feel abandoned in prayer, let us be aware the lack is not in God but in us—in our health, in our mind, in our circumstances, in the way we're behaving, or in the nature of the state of prayer we have reached. There are states of prayer in which we feel a sense of the absence of God that is not God's absence, but absence of thoughts, feelings, emotions about God—and none of these ever was God, but only ways of registering God's presence. They sometimes fail us, but God never fails us.

Jesus, dying, losing his mental powers, perhaps experienced this terror known to the mystics. St. Augustine may be suggesting this when he asks: "What part of him hung on the cross if not the part he received from us? How could God the Father ever cast off or abandon his Son, who is indeed one God with him? ... Christ cried out with the very voice of humanity"[6] In St. Paul's words, "He emptied himself" (Ph 2:7). He is sharing to the full what he became in becoming one of us. He is taking on the burden of dying with us and like us. He shared our depths of dereliction, crying out in his voice for all the abandoned of all time.

Let us be comforted by this, that feelings can deceive and mislead us; that if Jesus could feel abandoned, we need not fear that all is lost when we feel abandoned. Rather, let us feel free to cry out to God with Jesus, "My God, my God, why have you forsaken me?" Let us not be afraid to pray like Jesus, for we want to be like Jesus in all things.

---

[6] *Divine Office*, 2nd reading for Tuesday, 2nd week of Lent.

The Sixth Word

IT IS FINISHED

The sands of time are running out for Jesus. The important people on Calvary view him as a disgrace, a condemned criminal who claimed to be Someone, but whose claim is bankrupt now.

Many a modern gives the same assessment. A priest beginning a talk to a group of school children sized up their restlessness and utter unreadiness to listen to spiritual talk. He realized they were taken in by television and misled by the inanities and false values of the world. How can he reach them with the mystery of Christ?

He sensed the cause of their resistance and decided to bring it into the open. He asked bluntly, "Was Christ a success or a failure?" A boy hardly in his teens responded: *He was a failure. People rejected him, his apostles ran away, and they killed him.* Now the youngsters' concern and confusion was addressed. They fell silent and listened.

We listen, too, for Jesus' next word. Will he address this issue thick around him on Calvary and thick around us today? Will he give God's measure of success? Will he open his Heart once more, and speak a word by which he himself weighs and assesses the life he has just spent on earth?

The soldiers wet his lips with a sponge dipped in wine, and Jesus says, "It is finished" (Jn 19:30).

It is finished? What is he saying? Is he saying, "At last I'm out of it. At last the suffering is over"?

Tetelestai, the Greek word in John's Gospel that is translated "It is finished," tells us far more clearly than the English translation what Jesus means. A story will convey his meaning. You've planned your dream house, hired an architect and a contractor and can't wait until the work is done. Suddenly you are called out of town. Finally, anxiously, you return. You aren't even unpacked when the doorbell rings. Your contractor is standing there. He hands you the keys and says triumphantly, "It is finished." That is the meaning of the word Jesus uses.

Tetelestai means that the intended goal, the objective, the purpose has been reached. A cognate Greek word bearing a closely related meaning has been transported into English in the word *entelechy*. Entelechy is the dynamism in a living thing which moves it towards its purpose and its fullness, in accord with the saying of philosophers, "Everything that acts, acts for a purpose."

A little acorn hangs from a tree, a living thing, a seed. It falls to the ground, blows about in the winds and the rains, is buried in leaves and soil and begins to germinate. The entelechy is at work. Roots go down, a spear comes up, a sapling rises. Thirty years later there stands a noble oak tree. If it could speak it might say, "It is finished. I have done it!" The entelechy has worked itself out.

This is what Jesus is clearly saying. The soldiers recognized that cry of a conquering warrior, as their later exclamation of faith would indicate: "Surely this was the Son of God!" (Mt 27:55).

The purpose of my coming, Jesus is saying, *has been realized. I have reached my goal of doing my Father's will. As by one man's disobedience all became sinners, by my obedience all will be made just.*[7] *The prophecies have been fulfilled. The work of redemption has been completed. I've done it! It is consummated!*

That sentence, *It is consummated,* is the better translation of the Greek word *tetelestai*. It is the phrase used of a marriage after the bride and groom have united on their marriage bed. On his bed of the cross, Christ consummated his marriage with his Church-to-be. He has not only taken flesh, he has lived human life to the full in loving, in giving, in serving, in daring, in boldness and endurance to the very end. He even delays his resurrection for three days to assure us beyond a doubt that he has shared death with us as well.

The path to this consummation of his purpose on earth is a life of obedience to his Father.

The Letter to the Hebrews tells us that "When he came into

---

[7] See Romans 5:19.

the world he said, 'As is written of me in the scroll, Behold, I come to do your will, O God'" (Heb 10:5, 7). As a boy in the Temple he said, "Didn't you know I must be about my Father's work?" (Lk 2:49). Later, he said, "My food is to do the will of the One who sent me, and to finish his work" (Jn 4:34).

At the Last Supper he said, "Father, I have finished the work you have given me to do" (Jn 17:4). Now he has finished the suffering as well. He has fulfilled all the prophecies, and made good on all God's promises. And in all of this, by word and work, he has ringingly proclaimed what constitutes success in life and what constitutes failure.

We stand in spirit with Christ while he consummates his work as Redeemer, but it remains for us to consummate our share in the work and the suffering.

Obedience to God is the one and only way to reach the point where we can say with Jesus, "It is finished." Mary told us as much at Cana: "Do whatever he tells you" (Jn 2:5). We owe obedience to God in and through his Church by fulfilling our purpose, our vocation, our meaning as humans and as this particular person by living, growing, loving, serving, building and bearing the consequences. That is why the Daily Offering of the Apostleship of Prayer is so fine a thing. Each day we promise to walk in the footsteps of Jesus, doing the Father's will as life presents it daily.

Suffering is not a virtue; it is the price of faithfulness in a sinful world. Like Jesus, we go our way as man, woman or child, making use of the talents and opportunities God gives us, going straight forward in faith, conviction, and commitment, bearing the onslaught of those who would have us follow another way, the so-called easy way of the world, the way of evil, of sin, of Satan.

Is the priesthood or religious life difficult? Then leave it. Does your spouse mistreat you? Find another. Would this child be an inconvenience? Well, you know about abortion.

Such is the way of the world, but the way of Christ is fidelity. The truly wedded become one flesh until death do them part. Priests and religious follow Christ to the end.

No more than Jesus do we make suffering our purpose. Jesus did not crucify himself. Our purpose is to fulfill God's will for us, and bear the consequences even to martyrdom as Jesus did. That is the successful way of life, and no other. "Thy kingdom come, thy will be done."

We celebrate this way of life with Jesus in the Holy Sacrifice of the Mass. The Mass is nothing but love's never-ending story, the story of Calvary told and retold, lived and relived, our story entwined with it. "No one has greater love than this, to lay down one's life for one's friends" (Jn 15:13). Jesus is present, risen, the high priest at each Mass, sharing his life with us and offering his five wounds to the Father for us, and so offering Calvary still. By our daily offering of our lives, we fill up the mystery of the Mass. Our life and sufferings are on the paten with him, so that one day we too can say on our deathbed those glorious words, "It is finished."

FATHER, INTO YOUR HANDS
I COMMEND MY SPIRIT

In spirit we are with Jesus on his deathbed, the cross. He is about to breathe his last. He who said, "Out of the abundance of the heart the mouth speaks" (Mt 12:34), will speak once more. Let us listen intently, for this is his last chance to speak his Heart.

Lips open, and there comes forth the loud cry, "Father, into your hands I commend my spirit!" (Mk 23:46). Do you recognize that his last word sums up his whole life? The Gospels make it clear that his divine Father is the heart of his Heart.

One day a five-year old boy asked his father why he didn't know his grandfather. The father explained to his child for the first time that he himself had been raised in a home, deprived of a father. The child, sobbing uncontrollably, said he couldn't imagine the sadness of not having a father. What then of the more unimaginable sadness of not knowing God our Father? Jesus spent his whole life teaching us to know God his Father and ours.

Once a crucifix slipped from a pedestrian's hand, and fell into a trench. A workman located it, returned it to her, told her she was lucky she had faith, and said he was a Jew and had none. She urged him to pray. He replied that his mother had taught him to pray, but now there remained only the one prayer which he prayed each night: "Into your hands I commend my spirit."

The words are from Psalm 31, verse 5, the very words Jesus cries in this last moment. Surely they were taught to him, too, by his Jewish Mother, Mary. Jesus, however, added to the phrase one most important word which is central to his teaching: *Father*. "Father," Jesus cried, "into your hands I commend my spirit."

The Greek word translated *commend* also means *to entrust, to set before as a meal*. The meaning fits, for when Jesus breathed his last, he went home to the Father, who will feast on his Son's presence forever.

But before we think of the Father's joy in his Son's homecoming, can we be so heartless as not to think of his sorrow at his Son's torment? Since God speaks in the Scriptures in human ways of his sorrow because of human sin and suffering, it is certainly not forbidden us to imagine his grief as he gazes at his Son dying. The beloved King David's grief on losing his son Absalom symbolizes the Father's grief. As we have rebelled against the Father by sin, Absalom, lusting to be king, rebelled against his father. He fomented a civil war to seize the kingdom. David ordered his generals not to harm his son. They killed him anyway, ending the war. David the victor did nothing but weep that day, saying, "My son Absalom! Absalom! My son, my son!" (2 S 19:5). At last his officers told him that instead of thanking his troops for winning the victory, he was making them slink around shamefacedly. For his faithful followers's sake the king dried his tears.

What of Jesus's Father? If he acted like a human father he would drench the world in tears. Wasn't the first deluge God weeping over his world gone astray? What a deluge there ought to be now! But the Father hides his tears lest we, ashamed and afraid, slink away. He will not ruin the work of his Son, who died to lead us home to the Father, knowing that *the Father loves us as he loves his Son.*

Is that hard to believe? At the Last Supper, praying to the Father for his followers, present and future, Jesus petitioned "that the world may know that you sent me, and that you loved them as you loved me" (Jn 17:23). So King David, the bereaved father, stands as a scriptural symbol of the eternal Father, who, hiding his tears, accepts Jesus's sacrificial offering for our salvation.

Jesus spoke his last mortal word and died. It is time to look at the joyful side of its meaning for Jesus.
The English Cardinal Manning, on his deathbed, was asked how he felt. "Like a schoolboy," he said, "going home for the holidays." That is a sentiment not unworthy of the Heart of Jesus. Heaven is his home and ours. He longed to go home, to leave rejection, terror, horror behind. Speaking of death as a "baptism," he said,

"There is a baptism with which I must be baptized, and how great is my anguish until it is accomplished!" (Lk 12:50). What joy we should feel for him! His earthly work is done, his sufferings ending, his victory won.

What joy for him that now, as he said at the Last Supper, "I am going to prepare a place for you... so that where I am you also may be" (Jn 14:2-3). He is achieving what he came to do: lead us to the Father.

When will he return for us? There was an ancient Jewish custom that throws light on this. When a couple became engaged, the bridegroom-to-be went home and began to build a lodging on his father's property. Only when his father said, "Your abode is now ready," could the son go for his bride. That custom seems the best explanation for Jesus' words about the end-time and his return: "Of that day and hour no one knows, neither the angels of Heaven, nor the Son, but the Father alone" (Mt 243:36). Jesus remains at home with the Father, preparing for his bride the Church, waiting for his Father to say, "Go now, get your bride."

But let us return to Jesus on Calvary. After he lets his head fall upon his breast and breathes forth his spirit, they pierce his side, and blood and water flow out. It looks like mere butchery, but in God's providence it is one of the most meaningful events of all time. John's Gospel recalls it with such solemnity and such references to prophecies of the event that it has been called *the sign of salvation!*

Jesus himself spoke solemnly of the meaning of his crucifixion: "When you lift up the Son of Man, then you will realize that I AM" (Jn 8:28). I AM was God's Name in late Jewish tradition (See NAB, footnote on Jn 8:24, 28). Moses, by God's order, lifted up the brazen seraph serpent in the desert to heal people bitten by seraph serpents (Nb 21:4-9). Jesus presents himself as the new cure that God is providing for the bite of sin which is eternal death. The cure is God himself on the cross.

Elsewhere Jesus had said, "When I am lifted up from the earth, I will draw everyone to myself" (Jn 12:32). This is often taken to refer to Jesus being lifted up in resurrection. That is no doubt included, but resurrection without the cross might never have stirred hearts or awakened faith. What the Church has learned through the ages is that the Pierced One hanging on the cross in truth has drawn uncounted sinners to him in tears to be healed. The power of the Pierced One and his pierced Heart is no less than the power of God who is Love, pouring out his love to a love-famished world. It is both the sign and the power of salvation.

This divine, transforming power and love continue to pour into the world every day, for the daily Mass and Eucharist and Calvary and Last Supper are all substantially and mystically one; and if we join ourselves to it, as in the Daily Offering or any similar way, we are "as it were at the foot of the cross with Mary, united with the offering and intercession of Christ," and all the more so when we are at Mass (see CCC #1370; and #1367-8).

Now, at the piercing of your Heart, there is set before us the moment you spoke of, Jesus, when you cried, "Let anyone who thirsts come to me and drink. Whoever believes in me, as scripture says: 'Rivers of living water will flow from within him'" (Jn 7:37-38). Here now is the Jordan of baptism and the river of Eucharistic blood, given for the rebirth and nourishment of your body the Church, the new Eve, present symbolically in Mary, in whose arms your body will be laid, and washed with the pure water of her tears (Cf. Evangelium Vitae, #50-51).

We speak and say, "Jesus, they can't hurt you, we can't hurt you any more. We're so glad. But we know also, Jesus, that your Father wouldn't let anything happen to you or be taken from you that he couldn't restore in a more glorious way."

The Psalms call you the fairest of the sons of men. Your wounded body is fair and noble even in death, but in three days it will be glorious beyond our dreams. The Father let you do battle knowing you would triumph. Others would sin against you but you would not sin in return. Others would use violence against you but you would never be violent. And so you conquered in accord with your declaration, "Take courage, I have overcome the world" (Jn 16:33). Yours is the victory and so many fail to see it. Give us the word and the prayer, Lord, to spread the faith.

Finally, we reflect on the meaning of Calvary for ourselves.

If we are bold enough to say it, though it sounds like madness to the world, our sufferings are toothless monsters, not worthy to be compared with the glory that awaits us. Jesus told us not to be afraid of those who can harm the body. God can restore it to eternal life, to a glory it has never known. Life, he taught us, is a time of serving and growing and loving and giving and preparing for dying. Death is our true birth. In death, life is changed not taken away. Joy is ahead in eternal life.

In the venerable old wedding instruction, the couple were told that "the future with its... joys and sorrows, is hidden... These elements are mingled in every life.... The rest is in the hands of God. Nor will he be wanting to your needs." This instruction applies to the lives of us all.

Eternal Father, at every Eucharist you give us your pledge of eternal life, your Son's risen body and blood. It is the pledge that nothing is lacking to us. We are in your hands, Father. We need only respond. No one can take from us what really counts unless we plunder ourselves by sin. Help us to pray nightly, and at the hour of our death, "Father, into your hands I commend my spirit."

Chapter Seven

HIS SPECIAL WORKS

SAVING THE UNBORN TO THE GLORY OF GOD
THE PRO-LIFE LEAGUE OF THE HEART OF JESUS

SAVING THE UNBORN
TO THE GLORY OF GOD

The failure of the vast effort to save most of the dying unborn compels a question: Is our anti-abortion strategy faulty? What is our pro-life effort failing to do?

Is there a more effective strategy to counter what Vatican II called an unspeakable crime? Since pro-life work moves us into action at the heart of society, we should find help to answer those questions in the Spirit-inspired political strategy of Pope Leo XIII. Living in troubled, changing times, he "carried the Church chronologically and intellectually into the 20th century" by applying Catholic principles to social problems. He produced "the foundations of modern Church social teachings." In 1991 we celebrated the centenary of his social encyclical, *Rerum Novarum, On the Condition of the Working Class*.[1]

But it was *Annum Sacrum (Holy Year)*, his encyclical of May 25, 1899, that the Pope himself called "the greatest act of my pontificate."[2] By it he ordered Catholic churches worldwide to consecrate the whole human race, Christian and non-Christian, to Jesus Christ the King, to whom all belong, whether or not they acknowledge it or know it.

"Such an act of consecration," he stated, "since it can establish or draw tighter the bonds which naturally connect public affairs with God, gives to States a hope of better things. In these latter times es-

---

[1] See "Leo XIII: 'Lame Duck Pope Left Great Mark on Church'" (*Catholic Standard and Times*, 3/7/91), p. 10.
[2] *Sister Mary of the Divine Heart*, by Abbé Louis Chasle (London, Burns & Oates Limited, 1906), p. 375.

pecially, a policy has been followed which has resulted in a sort of wall being raised between the Church and civil society."

The result is that in government "the authority of sacred and divine law is utterly disregarded, with a view to the exclusion of religion from having any constant part in public life. This policy almost tends to the removal of the Christian faith from our midst, and, if that were possible, of the banishment of God Himself from the earth."

The result, the Pope teaches, is that the public welfare falls in on its foundation, and God leaves his enemies "the prey of their own evil desires, so that they give themselves up to their passions and finally wear themselves out by excess of liberty."

Recalling the conversion of Constantine by the sign of the Cross in the heavens and the military victory, promised then, that followed, the Pope calls us to trust in the heavenly sign of our day, "the most Sacred Heart of Jesus, with a cross rising from it and shining forth with dazzling splendor amidst flames of love. In that Sacred Heart all our hopes should be placed, and from it the salvation of men is to be confidently sought."[3]

Pope Leo's teaching helps us to turn our questions into another question that implies its own answer: Is not the pro-life movement failing to put all hope in God Incarnate rather than in human efforts? Trust in our efforts is secularist, and doomed. Leo XIII trusted not in his labor encyclical, but in the Heart of the Savior flaming with love for his world.

The love of the Heart of Jesus for his unborn ones needs to be our hope. To Jesus we ought to consecrate all our efforts. This will constitute a new approach: We will expect success not from our efforts but from the divine favor. For all results we will give thanks to God, not to ourselves.

This was the strategy of Fr. Henry Ramiere, S.J., the "second founder" of the Apostleship of Prayer (the A.P.). His "epoch-making" book, *The Apostleship of Prayer*, was subtitled, "A League of

---

[3] *Annum Sacrum* in *The Papal Encyclicals: 1878-1903*, ed: Claudia Carlen (The Pierian Press, Ann Arbor, 1990), pp. 453-4.

Christian hearts united with the Heart of Jesus to obtain the salvation of the world and the triumph of the Church."[4] The book portrays in readily understood theological teaching his vision not only of worldwide salvation but of worldwide cultural transformation through the spread of the A.P.

Pope Pius IX approved the first A.P. Statutes in 1866, and Popes since then have urged all Catholics to join the Apostleship of Prayer. Pope Leo, and Popes since, have expressed an even fuller hope of a social and societal transformation through the spread of the Gospel. Pope Paul VI called this hoped-for new society "the civilization of love."

Pope Pius XII made an incisive observation about the A.P., quoted by Popes since: The Apostleship of Prayer "is not merely one of prayer" because it stimulates all to fulfill the command of love of neighbor, and it "stirs a complete giving of self out of love for God and men. How appropriate is the League's motto, 'Thy kingdom come'!"[5]

This is borne out in the nature of the Daily Offering: It is a *prayer to be lived in total self-giving to the Son by the guidance of the Holy Spirit.* A Morning Offering lived out and guided by an Evening Examen is a serious apostolic way of life. Each member gives all, each in his or her own way. Each is kept on track by the Examen and by growth in contemplation in action. These spiritual practices are capable of guiding a member in affairs large and small in his or her life— including vocation, career choice, and daily decisions.

The A.P. is a precision instrument to help people answer Pope John Paul II's summons to engage in the new evangelization — an evangelization which cannot do without pro-life efforts. In his 1997 message for the World Day of Prayer for Vocations, the Pope stated: "As I have often recalled, this is the time of the new evangelization in which everyone is involved. In an ever more secularized world, a renewed 'implantation of the Church' is to be courageously promoted

---

[4] *The Apostleship of Prayer* (Messenger of the Sacred Heart, Philadelphia, 1889), vi-vii.
[5] Letter of 9/19/48 to the General of the Society of Jesus.

as the condition which is always necessary so that the vocational experience might be possible."

In *Crossing the Threshold of Hope*, the Pope says that Vatican II originated the "new evangelization," but that the term "was popularized by Pope Paul VI's *Evangelii Nuntiandi* as a response to the *new challenges that the contemporary world creates for the mission of the Church.*" In 1991 Pope John Paul II wrote his *Redemptoris Missio* which "represents a new synthesis of the Church's teaching about evangelization in the contemporary world."[6] In this encyclical the Pope teaches that "Building the Kingdom means working for the liberation from evil in all its forms. In a word, the Kingdom of God is the manifestation and realization of God's plan of salvation in all its fullness" (#15).

The new evangelization puts up front the unnegotiable call of Jesus to care for him in his brethren in hunger, nakedness, and, it would seem, every need. This is not a substitute for preaching the Gospel, but an element at its core: If not preached by love, the Gospel is not preached in truth. "The challenge of the new evangelization," says the Pope, "demands that the saving message permeate human hearts and society's structures."[7] That mandates the involvement of each and every Christian in this evangelization, for only Christians as a whole can permeate the whole of human society.

That is why the Pope calls on the Apostleship of Prayer to go into action with its tens of millions of members. "It is obvious how urgent it is for members of the Apostleship of Prayer to be involved in the service of the new evangelization," he says, and adds: "The new evangelization will also be effective insofar as it strengthens the bonds of ecclesial communion with the grace that flows from the Heart of Christ. The Apostleship of Prayer during the past century and a half has created a profound communion of prayer among hun-

---

6 *Crossing the Threshold of Hope.* See pp. 160 and 105-117.
7 "To Latin Religious Toward the Fifth Centenary of New World Evangelization" (*Origins*, vol. 20: No. 13), p. 215.

dreds of millions of believers. Nothing less is expected of it in the future."[8]

To experts in the Apostleship of Prayer, it is obvious that to support the new evangelization, the A.P. needs to found new sections according to its statutes and custom, to bring people together to deal with new social needs and crises. Who has a greater need or a greater crisis than the millions of children about to be slaughtered in the womb, and even as they leave the womb, in the so-called partial birth abortion, which is clear and simple infanticide, the other crime which Vatican II called *unspeakable*.

A new section of the Apostleship of Prayer to restore civilization's reverence, respect, and legal protection for the unborn was founded as a special contemporary service of the A.P. Both current and new members are called to join the new section, for a vast army deployed in every walk of life is required to serve life. The Statutes for the Pro-Life League of the Heart of Jesus, the new section of the Apostleship of Prayer, follow. They explain how to collaborate with the Heart of Jesus to begin and carry on this save-the-children work in a new vein, expressly to the glory of the Heart of Jesus, for the advance of the Civilization of Love, **AMDG.**

---

[8] "Pray for the Urgent Needs of the Church" (*L'Osservatore Romano*, Dec. 21/28, 1994), p. 7.

STATUTES OF
THE PRO-LIFE LEAGUE OF THE HEART OF JESUS

(© Copyright 1996; revised 12/16/98, Apostleship of Prayer,
3 Stephan Avenue, New Hyde Park, NY 11040)

Preamble

The Pro-Life League of the Heart of Jesus is a *section* of the Apostleship of Prayer. A *section* is composed of members who add to the Apostleship's purpose a special goal that brings them together.

The Apostleship of Prayer (*A.P.* for short) is a worldwide association of the faithful united by prayer and apostolic purpose. By their Daily Offering members "unite themselves with the Eucharistic Sacrifice, in which the work of our redemption is continuously accomplished." They believe that "this vital bond with Christ" alone makes any apostolate productive. By this vital bond, they "cooperate in the salvation of the world" (*A.P. Statutes* I).

I. PURPOSE OF THE PRO-LIFE LEAGUE

Guided by faith, members profess with Pope John Paul II that "The Church is called upon to manifest anew to everyone, with clear and stronger conviction, her will to promote human life by every means and to defend it against all attacks in whatever condition or state of development it is found."[1]

The purpose of the Pro-Life League of the Heart of Jesus is to promote the reign of his Heart by supporting the rights of the pre-born child. Members are mindful that the Heart they honor

---

[1] Pope John Paul II, Apostolic Exhortation, *On the Family*, #30.

once beat in the breast of a defenseless unborn child under the Immaculate Heart of his Mother. They desire to honor him in every
child to whom their help reaches. And they are moved to action by
the utter defenselessness of the pre-born child. They work to assist
every mother, every father, and every person to recognize, cherish
and protect the life of every human person in as well as out of the
womb.

The League professes that to glorify God we must keep his
commandments, showing we have always at heart his power and
greatness.[2] These shine out in the marvels God works for his human
family, for "they glorify the Lord who are alive and well" (Sirach
17:23). Because he loves all mankind, God declares, "Thou shalt not
kill." The glory of God's creation is darkened by flagrantly disobey-
ing this law of love and depriving an innocent human being of life.
In light of the Incarnation, the sin and crime is even worse, for "by
his Incarnation the Son of God has united himself in some fashion
with every person." Thus, "rejection of human life, in whatever form
that rejection takes, is really a rejection of Christ." This especially
includes every helpless baby whose life is threatened.[3]

**The League teaches with Pope John Paul II that "prayer
joined to sacrifice constitutes the most powerful force in history."[4]** The League teaches that we will not make due progress in
protecting the unborn until we rely unreservedly on God's Incarnate
Son, and make it evident that the praise for any success goes to him
and his Virgin Mother. Jesus is, after all, the "Author of life" (Acts
3:15). Mary, in her divinely appointed role, is "a mother of all who
are reborn to life. She is in fact the mother of the Life by which everyone lives."[5] Her *Magnificat* sets us an example of giving God the
glory.

---

[2] St. Bede wrote that "observance of God's commands shows that (a person) has God's
power and greatness always at heart" (*The Divine Office*, Feast of the Visitation, second
reading).

[3] See *Evangelium Vitae*, #104.

[4] Pope John Paul II, General Audience, Jan. 12, 1994; quoted in *The Catholic Standard
and Times*, 8/4/94, p. 8.

[5] Blessed Guerric of Igny, quoted by Pope John Paul II in *Evangelium Vitae*, #102.

Giving this glory to life's Author requires prayer and action. We cultivate daily prayer, attitudes and activities that generate reverence for the child in the womb, and for all human life. We reverence human life from fertilization to natural death. We oppose both abortion and euthanasia. We believe the soul "is immortal: it does not perish when it separates from the body at death, and it will be reunited with the body at the final resurrection."[6]

All is to be done in union with and through the Immaculate Heart of Mary, Mother of Christ our Life. Members imitate her "who is so intimately associated with the work of the redemption" (*A.P. Statutes* II, 3).

The League's doctrine and conduct are guided by the Vicar of Christ on earth. It promotes his monthly Prayer Intentions for Church and world. It fosters penance and reparation by prayer, fasting and love in action to build up the "civilization of love," the "Kingdom of the Heart of Christ," which alone will establish a pro-life culture.[7]

The founding and forwarding of the League will depend on those who believe and meditate on the words of the Author of Life that "without me you can do nothing" (Jn 15:5). League members say *Amen* to Pope John Paul II's declaration that "a great prayer for life is urgently needed, a prayer which will rise up throughout the world."[8] For "If the Lord does not build the house, in vain do its builders labor" (Ps 127:1).

In this spirit of reverence for God, absolute Master of life, we are inspired to work and cooperate with all who reverence him and every human being he creates, and with all who reverence life even if they do not yet know life's Author.

---

[6] *Catechism of the Catholic Church*, #366.

[7] For Church teaching on penance and reparation see the *Catechism of the Catholic Church*, ##1434-1439, 1505, 1969.

[8] *Evangelium Vitae*, #100.

II. RELATIONSHIP TO THE APOSTLESHIP OF PRAYER

**All members of the *Pro-Life League of the Heart of Jesus*
are members of the A.P., of which it is a section.** They are obligated to its spirit and practices. Pope John Paul II has specified the
main purpose of the Apostleship of Prayer. It is "to spread among
all the faithful the awareness of collaborating with Christ the Redeemer through the offering of their own lives united and lived with
the Heart of Christ in total consecration to his love and in reparation
for the sins of the world." He adds that "The promotion and vivifica-
tion of this essential spirit must constitute the *raison d'être* of the
whole organization, structure and activity of the Apostleship of
Prayer at this time."[9]

The basic duties are to say the Daily Offering in the spirit of
union with the Holy Sacrifice of the Mass, and to recite the rosary,
or at least a decade, daily. Members are urged, but not obligated, to
daily Mass and Holy Communion when possible (*A.P. Statutes* II,
1 and 3).

Pro-Life League members must realize, then, that "The primary purpose of even a Section must be to train its members in the
apostolic spirit, so that they may learn to make their whole life a
sacrifice in Christ and with Christ" (*TPG*, 197).[10]

Beyond that, *Pro-Life League* members aim, in union with the
A.P., to consecrate themselves and to inspire others to consecrate
themselves to the Heart of Jesus. This leads to returning love for love
in the spirituality of the heart as it is taught by the Church (*A.P. Statutes* II, 2).

Pro-Life League members carry out their pro-life work, then,
"in such a way that it is clear that it is undertaken especially in honor
of the Sacred Heart, and performed under his protection with the
intention that the success of the work may redound to the Glory of

---

[9] *L'Osservatore Romano*, 25 April 1985, page 5, #4; reprinted in *Prayer and Service*, 1985,
No. 4, p. 258. See also *1968 Statutes of the Apostleship of Prayer*, V.

[10] The Apostleship of Prayer, *A Theological and Pastoral Guide* (Central Office of the
Apostleship of Prayer, Rome, 1958), p. 197. When further material is drawn from this
source it will be identified *only by TPG and page number.*

the Sacred Heart of Jesus," thus extending "the Reign of the Sacred Heart" (*TPG*, 198).

III. PROGRAM OF THE PRO-LIFE LEAGUE OF THE HEART OF JESUS

The Pro-Life League exists to pray and serve on behalf of the Right to Life of the pre-born. It has no intention of competing with or replacing existing pro-life organizations. It exists to supplement and assist them. Already in 1948, Pope Pius XII made the relevant point, which Popes since have reaffirmed. The Pope said that, although the Apostleship of Prayer, the League of the Heart of Jesus, already numbered 35 million members, this fact should not arouse in anyone "the impression that the League invades the harvest fields of others. Those who, with a certain divine impulse, laid the foundation of the League of the Sacred Heart long ago openly declared that they were not going to create new associations where others were already flourishing, but that they would only seek to share with other associations the fire of divine love and apostolic zeal.... Hence, all associations among the Faithful, and especially those which bear the honored name of Catholic Action, will unite themselves to Christ and one another more closely in the bond of love the more abundantly they draw from the League as from a fountain of *water springing unto eternal life.*"[11]

Those words of Pope Pius XII express well why Vicars of Christ for a century have urged every Catholic, but especially those in apostolic organizations, to join the A.P. In the March 27, 1968 Letter of Approbation of the Post-Vatican II Statutes of the Apostleship of Prayer, we read that "Other assistance of such strength and accessibility to all can scarcely be found for preparing and encouraging the faithful to think with the Church, to pray continuously, to be devoted to the apostolate and to be mindful at all times of that point of doc-

---

[11] "The Pope and the League of the Sacred Heart," Letter of Pope Pius XII to the General of the Society of Jesus (National Office of the Apostleship of Prayer), p. 2.

trine that is of the greatest importance in carrying out the apostolate: 'Neither the one who plants nor the one who waters is anything, but only God, who causes the growth'" (1 Cor 3:7).[12] Thus membership in the League reminds its members on whom they are to rely, and to whom to give the glory.

The guidelines for our spiritual and apostolic activities are these:

1. Say and live the Daily Offering in accord with the *A.P. Statutes*.

2. Make reparation to the Hearts of Jesus and Mary. Do penance. Offer prayer and Communions of Reparation for the "unspeakable crime of abortion." Add, to the end of the Daily Offering: "and for reverence for human life in the womb."

3. Make at least the brief evening Examen of Conscience recommended to all Christians.[13] One reviews one's acts of commission and omission. Then one reviews one's personal response in the Holy Spirit to pro-life work, and expresses gratitude, sorrow, new resolve.

4. Inspire and support pro-life attitudes and apostolic activities in home and parish, in accord with the guidelines of the Bishop and sanction of the Pastor.

5. Individual members, if able and willing, should consider undertaking one or more of the following, or some similar activity the Holy Spirit may inspire:

   (1) Seek new members of the Pro-Life League, especially: a) among people whose health or occupation restricts their pro-life activity to prayer and sacrifice, and b) among post-abortion mothers and others formerly involved in abortion who long now to be fully reconciled with God, and who will willingly offer to the Heart of Jesus the words and works of reparation which are so much the purpose of the League.

   Father Peter-Hans Kolvenbach, the Director General of the Apostleship of Prayer, so aware that reparation takes

---

[12] For the Latin text of the letter see *Acta Romana Societatis Jesu*, vol. 15, pp. 203-205. The text quoted is found on p. 205.

[13] See the *Catechism of the Catholic Church*, ##1435 and 1452.

many forms, and that differing vocations and missions will lead different people to sanctify their sufferings and return Christ's love in differing ways, said aptly: "For some, it will be participation in the death agony of the Lord. For others, paschal joy and a look of hope capable of assuming and integrating all that is incomprehensible in the existential agony of men. For still others it will be the ardent faith which can build up the civilization of the Heart of Christ on the ruins accumulated through hatred and violence."[14]

(2) Promote membership in other pro-life organizations, including those dedicated to pregnant women in need of help.

(3) Join an existing pro-life organization in the parish, and participate in the prayerful spirit of the Pro-Life League.

(4) Where parish pro-life activities are absent, propose to the Pastor that they be started, and offer to help. Where they exist, promote a Pro-Life Day of Prayer and Fasting, or a workshop on right-to-life themes.

(5) Arrange an annual Pro-Life Retreat or Day of Recollection for members of the Pro-Life League and other interested persons.

(6) Use the media to forward Pro-Life League goals via letters, articles, airing views on radio and TV programs.

IV. FOUNDING A PRO-LIFE LEAGUE OF THE HEART OF JESUS

These *Statutes of the Pro-Life League of the Heart of Jesus* have been approved by the National Secretary as a special A.P. section for use in the United States, to meet present needs and circumstances, according to the urging of the *Statutes of the A.P.* (IV, 2, and V). They may be used in each diocese of the United States, once they have been approved by the Local Ordinary. Therefore the Local Director of the

---

[14] July 2, 1988 conference, "A Most Pleasant Mission," reprinted in *Prayer and Service*, 1988, Special Edition, pp. 34-5.

A.P. in any parish, school, retreat house or other center of the A.P. in such a diocese can establish this special section for those who wish to join. If the person in authority in a parish or school that is not yet a center of the A.P. wishes it to be become one, he or she need only apply to the Diocesan Director of the Apostleship of Prayer—or directly to the bishop if he has no Diocesan Director. Outside the United States, these Statutes must be approved by the National Secretary of the Apostleship of Prayer plus the Local Ordinary, before centers can adopt them.[15]

V. ENROLLMENT IN A PRO-LIFE LEAGUE

The Local Director of the A.P. has authority to enroll members in the A.P. and its local sections. If the Local Director appoints another to be director of the Pro-Life League section, authority to receive new members is also to be delegated (See *A.P. Statutes* IV, 5).

VI. MANAGING COMMITTEE, BYLAWS, AND A.P. CONTACTS

If the Local Director of the A.P. does not himself act as Director of the Pro-Life League, he will appoint or call for an election of a Director, along with a Secretary, Treasurer, and any other officers found necessary (*TPG*, 200). As the League develops, these officers will guide the drafting of bylaws to cover elections, frequency and times of meetings, dues, etc. With the pastor's approval, other specific commitments may be added, such as arranging an annual pro-life retreat open to all in the parish. Bylaws are subject to the approval of the Local Director. At meetings, individual members should report and discuss what they are doing in fulfillment of Part Three of these statutes.

---

[15] Beyond the U.S. borders, approval for use of these Statutes must also be sought from the Secretary General's Office in Rome. See *TPG*, 196-7 and *A.P. Statutes* V.

Remain in contact with the National Office of the Apostleship of Prayer, and the publications and religious goods it makes available (In the U.S.: Apostleship of Prayer, 3 Stephan Ave., New Hyde Park, N.Y. 11040 (516-328-9777). Maintain at least a communal subscription to the *Canadian Messenger of the Sacred Heart*. It serves all of North America (661 Greenwood Ave., Toronto, Ontario, Canada M4J 4B3).

Appendix One

PROCEDURE FOR ENROLLING IN
THE APOSTLESHIP OF PRAYER AT MASS

1. To reach the majority of the parishioners, the Enrollment Homily is preferably given at Sunday Masses. There is nothing controversial. The Apostleship of Prayer is not another organization, but an association in prayer and apostolic intent that Popes for a century have urged all Catholics to join. They do not exclude priests, religious, or members of other organizations, for as Pope Pius XII wrote, "We earnestly pray that all who are engaged in the external works of the apostolate belong to the Apostleship and be steeped in its spirit: clerics, and laity, men and women who in 'Catholic Action' or in other associations assist the hierarchical apostolates."

2. FOCUS: an intense personal devotion to the Heart of the Redeemer, aimed at daily prayer and total dedication of one's life in a sound apostolic way.

3. DAILY OFFERING CARDS (#203) are put in the pews before each Mass so people can pray the Daily Offering with the homilist during the homily, and take the prayer card home.

4. ENROLLMENT requires no signatures, dues, meetings or obligation under sin. (Those desiring to join stand and repeat a brief enrollment formula found in the homilies.)

5. PROMOTERS: It is recommended that the Pastor invite a few parishioners willing to act as Promoters to meet with him for a brief instruction on how to help keep the Apostleship vital in the parish. (See Statutes of the Apostleship of Prayer, Part III, in Appendix 3.)

6. If the parish is not already a Local Center of the Apostleship

of Prayer, the Diocesan Director of the Apostleship of Prayer—or the Ordinary, if he has not appointed a Diocesan Director—will enroll a parish or other center without charge. The Pastor may ask that another than himself—a priest, deacon or lay person—be appointed the local director. (See Statutes IV-3.)

RELIGIOUS GOODS

1. SACRED HEART AND IMMACULATE HEART OF MARY (IHM) PICTURES: To consecrate families to the Hearts of Jesus and Mary, a selection of pictures suitable for framing, with Family Consecration Leaflets, are made available. A small donation is requested to cover costs. (An opportunity for parishioners because, ordered singly from the National Office of the Apostleship of Prayer, they cost much more.) Books, pamphlets and holy cards, etc. are also put on sale. Supplies are ordered from the Apostleship of Prayer, 3 Stephan Ave., New Hyde Park, NY 11040 (1-516-328-6039). Phone for a Supplies List.

2. Copies of the *Canadian Messenger of the Sacred Heart* may be displayed, and information for ordering put in the bulletin. Messengers worldwide have been a most effective means of spreading the Devotion and keeping it alive. Here is a bulletin insert: Subscriptions to the SACRED HEART MESSENGER: $14.00 per year [1999 price]. Order from MESSENGER, 661 Greenwood Ave., Toronto, Ontario, Canada M4J 4B3.

Appendix Two

THE POPES

THE APOSTLESHIP OF PRAYER, THE LEAGUE OF THE HEART OF JESUS, IS FOR ALL CATHOLICS AND MEMBERS OF ALL ORGANIZATIONS

PIUS IX (1846-1878)

"The Apostleship of Prayer has always been especially close to the Roman Pontiffs. Pius IX approved its first statutes [in 1866] and exhorted its members to make the daily offering of their work and prayers for the intentions of the Church and the Pope."[1]

LEO XIII (1878-1903)

"Leo XIII issued nine different briefs conferring different privileges on the Apostleship."[2]

ST. PIUS X (1903-1914)

"The Catholics have established many very useful Works; but none is more useful than (the Apostleship of Prayer) of which you [the General of the Society of Jesus] are the Director General."[3]

---

[1] Letter of John Paul II to Father General of the Society of Jesus on the 150th Anniversary of the Apostleship of Prayer (*L'Osservatore Romano*, Dec. 21/28, 1994), p. 7.

[2] Louis Verheylezoon, S.J., *Devotion to the Sacred Heart* (Westminster, MD: Newman Press, 1955), p. 261.

[3] Quoted in Verheylezoon, p. 261.

BENEDICT XV (1914-1922)

"To all the faithful We strongly recommend the Apostleship of Prayer, expressing the wish that no one should omit joining it."[4]

POPE PIUS XI (1922-1939)

"Your apostolate is easy; and since it is available to all, the obligation urges beyond that of other forms of apostolic activity. Therefore all without exception should belong to it."[5]

POPE PIUS XII (1939-1958)

"We see with great satisfaction that besides the Society of Jesus …Bishops and very many secular and regular priests also, with a resolute will and united efforts, zealously endeavor to increase, support and direct this pious association."[6]

"We call the League (of the Sacred Heart, the Apostleship of Prayer) a perfect devotion to the Sacred Heart, so perfect that the two cannot be separated…. We, like Our Predecessor of happy memory, Pius XI, have made known and once more most willingly declare that it will make Us very happy if all the Faithful without exception enlist in this sacred militia to swell the army of Associates now numbering 35,000,000."[7]

"Nor can this arouse in anyone the uneasy impression that the League invades the harvest field of others. Those who, with a certain divine impulse, laid the foundation of the League of the Sacred Heart long ago openly declared that they were not going to create new associations where others were already flourishing, but that they

---

[4] Benedict XV, Apostolic Epistle *Maximum illud*, Nov. 30, 1919 (AAS, 11, 1919, 440-455). Quoted in Verheylezoon, p. 261.

[5] Pius XI: Address to Directors of the A.P., Sept., 1927. Quoted in Verheylezoon, p. 261.

[6] Letter to the Director General in 1944, the Centenary of the A.P. Quoted in Verheylezoon, p. 262.

[7] Letter of Pope Pius XII, Sept. 19, 1948, to Jesuit Father General John Baptist Janssens, on the occasion of a Conference of National Directors of the Apostleship of Prayer. Quoted from a copy issued by the National Office of the A.P.

would only seek to share with other associations the fire of divine love and apostolic zeal.

"Hence, all associations among the Faithful, and especially those which bear the honored name of Catholic Action, will unite themselves to Christ and one another more closely in the bond of love the more abundantly they draw from the League as from a fountain of water 'springing unto eternal life.'"[8]

"We ourselves are very familiar with the fruitful work of the Apostleship of Prayer. Out of zeal for souls and for the extension of Christ's Kingdom, We have recommended it many times to all.... If the Reverend Pastors will introduce the flocks committed to their care to the spiritual practices of the Apostleship of Prayer, they will satisfy no small part of their pastoral obligations."[9]

"We earnestly pray that all who are engaged in the external works of the apostolate belong to the Apostleship and be steeped in its spirit: clerics, and laity, men and women who in 'Catholic Action' or in other associations assist the hierarchical apostolates."[10]

POPE PAUL VI (1963-1978)

"His Holiness has by no means failed to note the importance of these new [1968] Statutes for more amply nourishing the spiritual and apostolic life of the members. Although it is not his intention to go into detail, nevertheless he cannot refrain from expressing open and particular praise for the close union with the Eucharistic Sacrifice which the members of the Apostleship of Prayer are asked to foster by means of the daily spiritual offering of themselves, so that the Sacrifice of the Mass may become the foundation and center of their lives. No one will fail to see how well this corresponds to the desire so insistently expressed by the Council (cf. *Constitution on the Sa-*

---

[8] The Letter of 9/19/48.

[9] Letter of Pius XII to Father General of the Society of Jesus, Oct. 28, 1951, given in full in *The Apostleship of Prayer: A Theological and Pastoral Guide 1958* (Central Office of the Apostleship of Prayer, Rome), pp. 3-6.

[10] Address of Pius XII at the Meeting of the A.P., Rome, Sept. 21-28, 1956. Translated from the address printed in *Nuntius Apostolatus Orationis*, Oct., 1956 (Central Office of the Apostleship of Prayer, Rome), pp. 281-284.

cred Liturgy, 48; *Dogmatic Constitution on the Church*, 11, 34; *Decree on the Ministry and Life of Priests*, 2, 5).

"Not less praiseworthy is the fact that the Apostleship of Prayer also stresses the devotion to the Sacred Heart of Jesus.... Eucharistic devotion, through which the whole life of the faithful is formed and disposed for perfect participation in the Sacred Liturgy... is richly nourished by devotion to the Sacred Heart of Jesus, that is, by knowledge of, devotion to, and imitation of the Divine Savior's love, 'who loved his own, who were in the world, to the end' (Jn 13:1)."

The new statutes "have given the Holy Father reason for greater esteem and benevolence toward this great family of people devoted to prayer, which without a doubt is to be numbered among the most salutary institutions which have arisen in the Church and are working for the Church...." He commends this devoted association "to all the children of the Church in whatsoever state of life they may be. Other assistance of such strength and accessibility to all can scarcely be found for preparing and encouraging the faithful to think with the Church, to pray continuously, to be devoted to the apostolate, and to be mindful at all times of that point of doctrine which is of the greatest importance in carrying out the apostolate: *neither he who plants is anything, nor he who waters, but God who gives the growth.*"[11]

"We think it your duty, your very life, to fulfill heartily the great vocation you have freely embraced, to spread always more and more, love for the Heart of Jesus.... For [Vatican II] has brought to light the brilliant mystery of the Holy Church. But this mystery can never be properly understood if the attention of the people is not drawn to that eternal love of the Incarnate Word, of which the wounded Heart of Jesus is the outstanding symbol; for as we read in the dogmatic Constitution which bears its name, 'The Church, or, in other words, the kingdom of Christ now present in mystery grows visibly through the power of God in the world. This inauguration

---

[11] *Letter of Approbation for the New Statutes*, March 27, 1968, from Cardinal Cicognani, the Secretary of State of His Holiness Paul VI, reprinted in *STATUTES of the Apostleship of Prayer (1968)*, General Office of the Apostleship of Prayer, Rome.

and this growth are both symbolized by the blood and water which flowed from the open side of a crucified Jesus.' (*On the Church*, #3). For the Church was born from the pierced Heart of the Redeemer and is nourished there.... Thus it is absolutely necessary that the faithful venerate and honor this Heart...."[12]

POPE JOHN PAUL II (1978—)

"A warm word of appreciation and of congratulation is addressed to the membership of the Apostleship of Prayer. Our conversation ought to be much more lengthy... given the fundamental importance of this Apostolate within the Church Universal as well as in the life of each and every one of the faithful."[13]

"The Apostleship of Prayer can bring a meaningful and concrete contribution to the diffusion, at all levels, of the great and consoling truth that all Christians can be intimately united to Christ the Redeemer by offering their own life to the Heart of Christ.... Thus will be accomplished Pius XII's hope that the 'Apostleship of Prayer... be so united to other pious Associations that it penetrates them like a breath of fresh air through which supernatural life and apostolic activity are ever renewed....' With these wishes I put this worldwide Pious Association into your hands as a precious treasure from the Pope's heart and the Heart of Christ."[14]

"The Apostleship of Prayer has always been especially close to the Roman Pontiffs. Pius IX approved its first statutes [in 1866] and exhorted its members to make the daily offering of their work and prayers for the intentions of the Church and the Pope. Every Pope since then has given special attention to this association, emphasizing the efficacious contribution it makes to apostolic activities.... The

---

[12] Pope Paul VI's letter to various religious orders, May 25, 1965, reprinted in *The Sacred Heart Encyclical of Pius XII, Haurietis Aquas* (Sacred Heart Publication Center, Orlando, FL) pp. 55-57. It is a complement to his apostolic letter of Feb. 6, 1965, *Investigabiles Divitias Christi*.

[13] *L'Osservatore Romano*, March 31, 1984.

[14] Address of Pope John Paul II to the Apostleship of Prayer, April 13, 1985 (*L'Osservatore Romano*, April 29, 1985, p. 5).

new evangelization will also be effective insofar as it strengthens the bonds of ecclesial communion with the grace that flows from the Heart of Christ."[15]

---

[15] Letter of John Paul II to Father General of the Society of Jesus on the 150th Anniversary of the Apostleship of Prayer (*L'Osservatore Romano*, Dec. 21/28, 1994, p. 7).

Appendix Three

Preamble

The Second Vatican Council laid strong stress on the fact that all the faithful are called to the apostolate. In order to fulfill this function, they are invited to take up external works and are urged to foster in themselves a vital union with Christ, and to nourish it in a special way through the liturgy and meditation on the Word of God. By performing their work according to the will of God, they can grow in that union. To this end the Council also gives special recommendation to associations which foster closer unity between their members' everyday lives and their faith, and also exhorts the laity to try with constancy to acquire the particular spiritual characteristics of their sodality or association. Just as former Statutes were repeatedly adapted to the needs of their own times, it was thought opportune to draw up new ones which would contain the teaching and spirit of Vatican II, and so adapt the Apostleship of Prayer to contemporary needs.

I. WHAT THE APOSTLESHIP OF PRAYER IS

Through baptism all the faithful share in the function of Christ as priest, king, and prophet, and are appointed by God to apostolic

activities in accord with their particular vocation. Within this universal apostolic vocation, the Apostleship of Prayer is a union of the
faithful who, by their daily oblation unite themselves with the Eucharistic Sacrifice, in which the work of our redemption is continuously accomplished and, by this vital bond with Christ, upon which
the fruitfulness of the apostolate depends, cooperate in the salvation
of the world.

Christ spread his kingdom by teaching and performing works
of mercy. At the same time, even from the very beginning he offered
his life to the Father for mankind, prayed for them, consummated
the offering of himself through the paschal mystery, and so redeemed
the world. In the same way every external apostolate ought to be
joined with prayer and sacrifice, so that it may contribute to the building up of the Body of Christ in the power of the sacrifice of the cross.

But this union with Christ the High Priest necessarily requires
an intimate bond with him through personal love. Therefore the
Apostleship of Prayer has given singular importance to the devotion
to the Sacred Heart of Jesus. Through it the faithful may reach more
deeply into the mystery of the love of Christ and so also share more
profoundly in the paschal mystery of the Lord. Through it they are
better able to respond to that love with which our Savior sacrificed
himself for the life of the world and from his transfixed Heart gave
life to the Church (Jn 19:34).

II. THE APOSTLESHIP OF PRAYER PROGRAM FOR THE
SPIRITUAL LIFE

For the exercise of their apostolic vocation, the Apostleship of
Prayer offers the faithful a program of apostolic spirituality whose
center is the Eucharistic Sacrifice.

1. The Sacrifice of the Mass and the Daily Offering

Since the Eucharistic Sacrifice is the source and apex of the
whole preaching of the Gospel, and the whole power of the Church's
activity flows from it, the spirituality of the faithful should also be

shaped by it. The Eucharistic Sacrifice should penetrate and form their lives and lead them to a conscious and vital participation in this mystery.

The Apostleship of Prayer insists, therefore, upon the daily offering, or oblation, by means of which a member offers himself through Christ to God—that is to say, offers all his prayers, actions, works, sufferings and joys—for the needs of the Church and indeed for the salvation of the whole world. This offering is described by the Council as follows:

> Besides intimately associating them [the laity] with his life and his mission, Christ also gives them a share in his priestly function of offering spiritual worship for the glory of God and the salvation of men. For this reason the laity, dedicated to Christ and anointed by the Holy Spirit, are marvelously called and equipped to produce in themselves ever more abundant fruits of the Spirit. For all their works, prayers, and apostolic endeavors, their ordinary married and family life, their daily labor, their mental and physical relaxation, if carried out in the Spirit, and even the hardships of life, if patiently borne—all of these become spiritual sacrifices acceptable to God through Jesus Christ (cf. 1 P 2:5). During the celebration of the Eucharist, these sacrifices are most lovingly offered to the Father along with the Lord's body. Thus, as worshipers whose every deed is holy, the laity consecrate the world itself to God (LG 34, 60).

This spiritual oblation, which pertains to the exercise of the common priesthood of the faithful, is at the same time also the exercise of their prophetic function, since it requires them to bear witness by their life, charity, labor, and apostolic activity. By living this daily oblation, the faithful bear witness to Christ before men and give testimony to the truth. This testimony of one's life, flowing from faith, hope, and charity, is the beginning of and the condition for all apostleship, and nothing can be found to put in its place.

Since, however, the Lord instituted the Eucharistic Sacrifice as a banquet, members, following the guidance of Vatican II, are not only to share in the Eucharistic Sacrifice frequently, and every day if possible, but should in it also receive the Body of the Lord, which is the sacrament of holiness, the sign of unity, and the bond of charity.

2. The Devotion to, or the Spirituality of, the Sacred Heart of Jesus

Christ not only gave up his life for us out of love (1 Jn 3:16), but also takes us up into the mysteries of his life and makes us a people set apart and a royal priesthood (1 P 2:9). We ought, therefore, to return him love for love. Since the Church teaches us that Christ's love is most particularly expressed through his Heart, and invites us to pay devotion to that love, symbolized in the Heart of Christ as the source of salvation and of mercy, the Apostleship of Prayer strongly urges its members to make themselves familiar with the practice and spirituality of devotion to the Heart of Jesus. They will respond to the Lord's love by consecrating themselves to him and practicing and fostering the forms of this devotion approved by the Church. They should imitate the example of Christ's love for his brethren and return the love of him who loved us with a human heart with the charity which is poured into our hearts by the Spirit.

3. Devotion to the Blessed Virgin Mary

Members of the Apostleship of Prayer are devoted with filial love to the Blessed Virgin Mary, the Mother of the Church, who is so intimately associated with the work of the redemption. They follow her example who devoted herself completely as handmaid of the Lord to the person and work of her Son. They should, therefore, make their offering of themselves to God through her who is our Mediatrix with her Son. They should recite the rosary, or at least one decade, daily, and earnestly commend the cares of the Church to her motherly heart. They should generously cultivate devotion to the Blessed Virgin Mary, and particularly in the liturgy, always remembering that a close union between the faithful and Christ is in no way hindered by the influence of his Mother, but is rather nourished by it.

4. Thinking with the Church

For the Church to carry out its task of uniting all men with Christ and among themselves, and to complete its work of building up his Body by the Eucharistic Sacrifice, all members must stir up in themselves and in others the desire to think with the universal Church and to share its concerns. For this purpose members make a daily offering for those intentions which the Supreme Pontiff proposes for the Apostleship of Prayer each month, or in urgent cases commends to the prayers of the faithful.

They will also readily include in their offering those intentions for which the bishops of their region request prayers.

5. Careful Attention to Prayer

Members are today aware that the human race is experiencing a new historical age, and is being shaken by profound and rapid changes and by deep disquiet. Therefore there is the greatest need of fervent and ceaseless prayer, that the world, liberated by the crucified and resurrected Christ, may, once the power of the Evil One has been broken, be transformed in accord with God's plans and reach its perfection.

Therefore members obey the Lord's command "to pray continuously and never lose heart" (Lk 18:1), and take seriously all things connected with cultivating the practice of prayer. Following the example of the Church, which continually takes up the bread of life from the table both of the Word of God and of the Body of Christ, members highly esteem the reading of Sacred Scripture and meditate on it. They cultivate sound mental prayer and various other forms of prayer, which they are free to choose for themselves. They should make days of recollection and retreats, which are excellent schools of prayer and of union with God in action, and they should foster these things in others.

III. THE ACTIVITY OF THE APOSTLESHIP OF PRAYER IN MODERN PASTORAL WORK

The Apostleship of Prayer offers services to pastors of souls and to the faithful, by which they form themselves for the apostolate and exercise it, and are also able to help any of the faithful to prepare themselves for the Christian life and the apostolate.

1. Training Promoters

Many of the members, known as promoters (the term varies according to local custom), are to be given special formation in the spiritual life in order to spread the Apostleship of Prayer and the apostolic spirit. The Apostleship of Prayer gives courses for biblical, spiritual, apostolic, liturgical, and ecumenical formation, in accord with the Council's Decree on the Apostolate of the Laity, Chapter 6. Thus formed by the deep spirituality of the Heart of Jesus, they should penetrate further into the mystery of Christ and learn to unite prayer and action, so as to be able not only to exercise the apostolate by the witness of their lives, but also to enable them to speak in such a way as to bring nonbelievers to Christ and to encourage the faithful to live lives of greater fervor.

2. Forms of Exercising the Apostolate

All members, but especially promoters, should foster everything connected with the spirit and program of the Apostleship of Prayer among those with whom they live, and make use of every means—including modern means of social communication—day by day to augment the practice of prayer and to deepen Christian life among the faithful. Priests and lay apostles should note that this spiritual program offers them a simple and effective means of helping themselves and others to lead good Christian and apostolic lives.

IV. THE STRUCTURE OF THE APOSTLESHIP OF PRAYER

1. The Apostleship of Prayer has its own structure, which is, however, to be adapted to various circumstances.

2. The Director General of the Apostleship of Prayer is the Father General of the Society of Jesus, who may delegate this function to another chosen by himself. He is aided in the exercise of this office in the various regions by National or Regional Secretaries, who are in charge of a whole country, or of a certain region, or of some works of the Apostleship of Prayer. They are appointed by the Director General, who takes account of whatever may be legitimately prescribed in respect to such appointments by the ecclesiastical authorities of the various countries.

3. One Diocesan Director is appointed in each diocese. If it seems opportune because of special conditions, there may be several. They should be priests, and be appointed by the Local Ordinary after notifying the National Secretary. The Diocesan Director sets up local centers and appoints local directors, who may be parish priests or other priests, or also religious, or lay people of either sex.

4. Both the Diocesan Director or Local Director and the National or Regional Secretary is to have a Lay Council, according to the circumstances of time and place, and according to local norms.

5. For a person to become a member of the Apostleship of Prayer, he is required either to be inscribed, or to give some other external sign to the local Director or to his delegate in order to show his desire for membership. The National Secretary, after hearing the opinions of those concerned, shall decide what means are to be chosen for this. In regard to promoters, however, the Directors are to take care that at least that form of organization required for exercising an orderly apostolate be kept in force among them.

6. To preserve unity of action and greater apostolic effectiveness, it is the duty of the National Secretary to see to the publication of periodicals, leaflets, and brochures for promoting the Apostleship of Prayer. The periodicals, under whatever title they may be published, should always fulfill the purposes of the Apostleship of Prayer and, at least on an inside page, indicate that they are periodicals of the Apostleship of Prayer.

V. SECTIONS OF THE APOSTLESHIP OF PRAYER

For the adaptation of the Apostleship of Prayer to the circumstances of the Church and of individual groups, it should contain special Sections, for example, those for youth, for men, for the sick, for Christian unity, and so on, which should be given titles of their own and be regulated by their own rules. New Sections, which do not go beyond the borders of their own countries, may be set up by the National Secretary with the consent of the Local Ordinary. Other Sections which do go beyond those borders, require approval from the Secretary General's office.

VI. APPROVAL OF THE STATUTES

Since the Statutes have been approved by the Holy See, they cannot be altered except by that same Authority. However, accommodations likely to be useful under certain local conditions, may be made with the approval of the Director General.

Approved by the Holy See on March 27th, 1968.

In April 1985, Pope John Paul II, expressing his "profound appreciation for, and great confidence in, the Apostleship of Prayer," confirmed these Statutes once again and gave his approval of them.

Appendix Four

JOB DESCRIPTIONS

Local Directors of the Apostleship of Prayer
Promoters of the Apostleship of Prayer

JOB DESCRIPTION: LOCAL DIRECTORS

Definition: A Local Director is a priest, religious or lay person
in a parish, school, retreat house or other center who has been au-
thorized to carry on the work of the Apostleship of Prayer (A.P.) by
the Diocesan Director of the A.P. (*Statutes of the A.P.*, IV-3). If he/
she is appointed by official title (e.g., as pastor, principal, etc.), the
role passes automatically to the person's successor; otherwise a new
appointment must be made. A Local Director may delegate another
to assist (IV-5). [Some elements in these guidelines are applicable
only to pastors or other priests, and must be read accordingly.]

1. *Basic Function*: The Local Director instructs and enrolls his/
her charges in the A.P., the League of the Sacred Heart. The A.P.
develops spiritual-apostolic life through saying and living the Daily
Offering. The Offering unites us with the Heart of Jesus in the
Sacrifice of the Mass. It consecrates our all, through union of mind
and heart with the universal Church, for the needs of the Church and
the world's redemption. It produces a loving, priestly, apostolic relationship with Christ in his whole life and mission (II-1). It nour-
ishes a filial love of the Blessed Virgin Mary, Mother of the Church
(II-3).

The reparation owed Christ includes a "repairing" of the de-
struction sin has worked on his creation, as in *The Spiritual Exercises*

of St. Ignatius, which inspired the A.P. "This is the true meaning of the reparation demanded by the Heart of the Savior—on the ruins accumulated through hatred and violence, can be built a civilization of love so greatly desired, the Kingdom of the Heart of Christ" (Pope John Paul II, 5/10/86).

2. *Enrolling Members*: At Sunday Masses, at least once a year, explain the A.P., and enroll new members and reactivate lapsed ones. There are no dues or name-taking. In the U.S., the following procedure suffices: After explaining the A.P., invite those who wish to join to stand and repeat the following formula: "LORD JESUS CHRIST, I WISH TO BECOME A MEMBER OF THE APOSTLESHIP OF PRAYER, THE LEAGUE OF THE HEART OF JESUS. I WILL SAY AND WITH YOUR HELP TRY TO LIVE THE DAILY OFFERING." THEN SAY, "I NOW ADMIT YOU AS MEMBERS OF THE A.P., THE LEAGUE OF THE HEART OF JESUS."

3. *Devotional Services*: Announce the monthly Holy Hour with benediction and exposition (and, if possible, confessions during the hour), and the First Friday Mass(es). [Pope John Paul II, observing that the Sacred Heart Devotion has "encouraged generations of Christians to pray more" and use the sacraments of Penance and the Eucharist, urges the continuation of the First Friday devotions, including the Holy Hour.] Some parishes conduct a Perpetual Friday Novena to the Sacred Heart of Jesus. The prayers are said at one Mass or a Mass/Holy Hour combination.

4. *Get Help*: Select and train *Promoters* to help carry on the work (III-1). Promoters are essential to the A.P.'s function and spread. Delegate Promoters to enroll new members, by visiting the sick, and giving talks in the schools, C.C.D., or other organizations (IV-5). A Promoter can see that the A.P. Monthly Intention of the Holy Father is published in the parish bulletin each month. An A.P. Lay Council helps with all this (IV-4).

5. *Conduct Formation Programs*: Give Promoters and all who are interested deeper formation in the spirituality, Scripture, and other theological dimensions of the A.P. Provide annual days of recollection and retreats in conjunction with other parishes. Be aware

that the Popes wish members of all other organizations to join the A.P. and be formed by its spirituality. The A.P. is not in competition with any other organization. It is not a movement but a spirituality with an apostolic thrust.

6. *Use the Services Provided by the A.P. Organization*: Ask the Diocesan Director if he is available to give Days of Recollection or a retreat in your parish open to all the parishes. Announce these in the diocesan newspaper.

7. *Parishes Include School*: You are also Local Director of any attached school. Instruction and enrollment of school children is one of the most effective A.P. works. See the National Office *list of supplies* for audio-visual aids.

8. *Promote Sacred Heart Literature and Art*: The National Office of the A.P., 3 Stephan Place, Hyde Park, NY 11040 (516-328-9777) has excellent supplies, including Pledge Cards, and large pictures with leaflets to consecrate the family to the Sacred Heart of Jesus. The *Canadian Messenger of the Sacred Heart* can be ordered from Messenger, 661 Greenwood Ave., Toronto, Ontario, Canada M4J 4B3. Read other Sacred Heart writings, such as Pope Pius XII's *Haurietis Aquas*, and John Paul II's *Pope John Paul II Prays The Litany*.

9. *Get Professional Help When Needed*: Ask the Diocesan Director, or a member of the Society of Jesus who specializes in the A.P., to conduct the enrollment talks at Sunday Masses.

10. *Know the A.P.'s Great Value*: Again and again, Popes have praised it for the spiritual and apostolic formation of the faithful. Pope John Paul II repeatedly urges its dissemination.

11. *The Responsibility for the Work Is Yours*: The Society of Jesus founded and supports the A.P., but only your Local Ordinary can appoint a Diocesan Director, who appoints Local Directors. At this point, priests, deacons, religious, and lay people are entrusted with the harvest. Being a good Local Director means using such guidelines as these judiciously. Do what you can of what they suggest, and inspire others to help. The Twelve Promises to St. Margaret Mary assure a rich harvest.

JOB DESCRIPTION: PROMOTERS

Definition: All members promote the A.P. *Promoters* are members who, by reason of greater zeal and native endowments, are appointed by the Local or Diocesan Director to render special services.

1. Promoters "are to be given special formation in the spiritual life." By formal courses, or by Days of Formation and Retreats, they are to be educated in biblical, spiritual, apostolic, liturgical and ecumenical matters, and in the spirituality of the Heart of Jesus. Thus they learn to unite prayer and action (See the *Statutes of the Apostleship of Prayer*, III-1. Study them!)

2. Promoters "should foster everything connected with the spirit and program of the A.P. among those with whom they live." Through personal contacts, deepen the prayer life of others. Capitalize, too, on any skills/expertise you possess for use of the media. Articles, interview opportunities on radio and TV, and even originating radio and TV programs, are all suggested activities for those with the competence (See III-2). Or simply, contact *The Sacred Heart Program*, 3900 Westminster Place, St. Louis, MO 63108 (314-533-0320), to learn of any radio-TV programs airing in your region. Try to list them in your parish bulletin and elsewhere.

3. Actions speak louder than words. Set an example by your life. Family comes first! No over-ambitious works. (To the A.P. Directors, Pope Pius XII said: "Everyone is not a good catechist or a good spokesman and proponent of the teachings of the Catholic faith.... Many too are so restricted by the care of the family which it is their vocation to establish, and which ought to hold first place, that they have neither means nor time at their disposal for the specific works of the apostolate.")

4. Your basic work is to spread the A.P., The League of the Sacred Heart, among the people in your own parish and school. Distribute the Daily Offering cards and the Holy Father's Monthly Intentions. Conduct meetings to discuss the A.P. (When funds are scarce some Promoters buy small supplies at their own expense.)

5. Submit inserts for your parish's weekly bulletin: the monthly intention, A.P. announcements, invitations to join the A.P., the

Daily Offering and other prayers to the Sacred Heart, etc. Submit appropriate selections to the diocesan paper, e.g., "Letters to the Editor" on apt issues. (Activities of Promoters should be coordinated under the Local Director. See IV-5.)

6. Since the Holy Father desires the practice of the monthly Holy Hour and the First Friday Mass of devotion to the Sacred Heart of Jesus, with Confessions, urge people to attend them.

7. Reach out to youth. Provide slide lectures and other opportunities to learn of the A.P. and the devotion to the Sacred Heart of Jesus. Seek opportunities to address catechetics classes on the A.P., or at least interest the teachers in doing so.

8. You may ask your Local Director of the A.P. to delegate you to enroll members in the A.P. Explain the A.P. to interested persons (the sick, the home-bound, etc), then ask him/her to repeat the following Enrollment Formula: "LORD JESUS CHRIST, I WISH TO BE A MEMBER OF THE APOSTLESHIP OF PRAYER, THE LEAGUE OF THE HEART OF JESUS. I INTEND TO MAKE AND LIVE A DAILY OFFERING." Then say, "I NOW ADMIT YOU AS MEMBER(S) OF THE APOSTLESHIP OF PRAYER."

9. The A.P. Statutes call for special sections "for example, for youth, for men, for the sick, for Christian unity, etc." (V). Offer your Local Director help for this. Invite the parish pro-life activists to form an A.P. Section, e.g., *The Pro-Life League of the Heart of Jesus*. Invite other groups to do the same, groups that are most in need of the divine help of the Heart of Jesus: parents, Natural Family Planning teachers and users, AIDS workers and AIDS victims, Charismatic Prayer Groups, etc.

10. Suggest to Eucharistic Ministers taking Holy Communion to the sick that they pass out Daily Offering cards, and even ask the Local Director to be delegated to enroll the Sick in the A.P.

11. Get to know the pictures, Sacred Heart badges, prayer cards and Home Consecration formulas, plus audio-visual aids, available from the Apostleship of Prayer, 3 Stephan Ave., New Hyde Park, N.Y. 11040 (Phone 516-328-9777). Distribute them. Promote consecration of each home to the Sacred Heart of Jesus and Immaculate

Heart of Mary, which families can perform—but it might encourage them if a Promoter offers to be present. Invite subscriptions to the *Canadian Messenger of the Sacred Heart*, 661 Greenwood Ave., Toronto, Ontario, Canada M4J 4B3. The popular Monthly Intention Leaflet is available from the National Office.

12. Inseparable from devotion to the Sacred Heart of Jesus is devotion to the Immaculate Heart of Mary (II-3). Promote the rosary and the First Saturday devotions.

13. These are suggestions. No one can do them all. Experience, prayer, discussion, and the Holy Spirit will guide you to what is realistic for you. Devotion to Jesus' Heart has been growing since St. John recorded his pierced side. The Lord told St. Margaret Mary he wants the devotion spread far and wide, and sent St. Claude de la Colombiere to her aid. Pray for their help in the work of the A.P., founded to do his will. Pope John Paul II said to the A.P. National Secretaries: "I put this worldwide Pious Association into your hands as a precious treasure from the Pope's heart and the Heart of Christ." Zealous Promoters are indispensable team members of the A.P. Do what you can.

Appendix Five

HEART OF JESUS NOVENA PRAYERS

Priest: In the name of the Father, and of the Son, and of the Holy Spirit. Amen.

All: Lord Jesus Christ, you have promised that where two or more are gathered in your name, you will be in the midst of them. Look down, then, with love and compassion upon us here before you to honor your Sacred Heart and to make it known and loved by all. Come into our midst, gentle Jesus, fill our hearts with blessings and inflame them with your love.

Priest: O Jesus, look upon those who kneel before you.

All: Heart of Jesus, hear and grant our prayers.

All: Divine Heart of Jesus, to you we have recourse. In you we find consolation when afflicted, protection when persecuted, strength when overwhelmed with trials and light in doubt and darkness.

We firmly believe you can bestow on us the graces we implore. We are most unworthy of your favors, but you are the God of mercies and will not refuse a contrite and humble heart.

Remembering your words: "Ask and you will receive, seek and you will find, knock and it will be opened to you"; mindful, too, that from your Sacred Heart have come words of tenderness and pleading love: "Come to Me, all you that labor and are burdened, and I will refresh you"; we come to you now with childlike confidence to make our pleas in this Novena. **(Pause here to make your petition.)** But, if what we ask is not for the glory of God and the saving of souls, answer our prayer in the way you know best. Whatever may be your decision with regard to our requests, we will never cease to adore, love and serve you. Amen.

Priest: O Jesus, answer our petitions as we kneel before you.
All: Heart of Jesus, hear and grant our prayers.

Priest: Let us pray.
All: O almighty and eternal God, look upon the Heart of your dearly beloved Son and upon the praise and satisfaction He offers you in behalf of sinners, and, being appeased, grant pardon to those who seek your mercy, in the name of the same Jesus Christ your Son, who lives and reigns with you in the unity of the Holy Spirit, one God, forever and ever. Amen.

SACRED HEART LITANY

Priest: Lord, have mercy on us.
All: Christ, have mercy on us.
Priest: Lord, have mercy on us. Christ hear us.
All: Christ, graciously hear us.
Priest: God, the Father in heaven,
All: Have mercy on us.
Priest: God the Son, Redeemer of the world,
All: Have mercy on us.
Priest: God, the Holy Spirit,
All: Have mercy on us.
Priest: Holy Trinity, one God,
All: Have mercy on us (Continue with the same response).

Heart of Jesus, Son of the Eternal Father,
Heart of Jesus, Formed by the Holy Spirit in the womb of the Virgin Mother,
Heart of Jesus, Substantially United to the Word of God,
Heart of Jesus, of Infinite Majesty,
Heart of Jesus, Sacred Temple of God,
Heart of Jesus, Tabernacle of the Most High,
Heart of Jesus, House of God and Gate of Heaven,
Heart of Jesus, Burning Furnace of Charity,
Heart of Jesus, Home of justice and love,

Heart of Jesus, Full of goodness and love,
Heart of Jesus, Perfection of all virtues,
Heart of Jesus, Most Worthy of all praise,
Heart of Jesus, King and Center of all hearts,
Heart of Jesus, in Whom are all the treasures of wisdom and knowledge,
Heart of Jesus, of Whose Fullness we have all received,
Heart of Jesus, Desire of the everlasting hills,
Heart of Jesus, Patient and most merciful,
Heart of Jesus, Enriching all who invoke Thee,
Heart of Jesus, Fountain of life and holiness,
Heart of Jesus, Sacrificed for our sins,
Heart of Jesus, Loaded down with reproaches,
Heart of Jesus, Bruised for our offenses,
Heart of Jesus, Obedient unto death,
Heart of Jesus, Pierced with a lance,
Heart of Jesus, Source of all consolation,
Heart of Jesus, Our Life and Resurrection,
Heart of Jesus, Our Peace and Reconciliation,
Heart of Jesus, Victim of sin,
Heart of Jesus, Salvation of those who trust in Thee,
Heart of Jesus, Hope of those who die in Thee,
Heart of Jesus, Delight of all the Saints,

Priest: Lamb of God, who takes away the sins of the world,
All: Spare us, O Lord!
Priest: Lamb of God, who takes away the sins of the world,
All: Graciously hear us, O Lord!
Priest: Lamb of God, who takes away the sins of the world,
All: Have mercy on us!
Priest: Jesus, meek and humble of Heart,
All: Make our hearts like unto thine!

Apostleship of Prayer with ecclesiastical approval (No. 253)

NOTE: Leaflets of this Novena to the Sacred Heart are available from the National Office of the Apostleship of Prayer (1-516-328-9777). Ask for Leaflet No. 253. There is also a Liturgical Novena in honor of the Heart of Jesus, No. 252.

MORNING OFFERING

O Jesus, through the Immaculate Heart of Mary, I offer you my prayers, works, joys and sufferings of this day in union with the Holy Sacrifice of the Mass throughout the world. I offer them for all the intentions of your Sacred Heart, the salvation of souls, reparation for sin, the union of all Christians. I offer them for the intentions of our bishops and of all apostles of prayer, and in particular for those recommended by our Holy Father this month.

Appendix Six

KEY BOOKS REFERRED TO IN THE TEXT

The Apostleship of Prayer, by Father Henry Ramière, S.J. (The Messenger of the Sacred Heart, Philadelphia, 1889. A new translation.) A revised edition was published in 1956 by The National Office of the Apostleship of Prayer, and De Nobili Press, Gujarat.

Behold The Pierced One, by Joseph Cardinal Ratzinger (Ignatius Press, San Francisco, 1986).

The Documents of Vatican II (America Press, New York, 1966).

Early Christian Doctrines, by J.N.D. Kelly (Harper & Row, Publishers, N.Y., 1978).

He Leadeth Me, by Walter Ciszek, S.J., with Daniel Flaherty, S.J. (Doubleday & Co, Inc., Garden City, N.Y., 1973).

The Letters of St. Margaret Mary Alacoque, transl: Clarence A. Herbst, S.J. (Henry Regnery Company, Chicago, 1954).

The Papal Encyclicals, ed. by Claudia Carlen (The Pierian Press, Ann Arbor, 1990).

Pope John Paul II Prays the Litany of the Sacred Heart of Jesus (Our Sunday Visitor Inc., Huntington, IN, 1992).

"Sign of Salvation: The Sacred Heart of Jesus," by Edouard Glotin, S.J., transl. by Carl J. Moell, S.J. (Apostleship of Prayer, New Hyde Park, 1990).

"Symbols, Devotions and Jesuits", a 60-page booklet in the series, Studies in the Spirituality of Jesuits (Studies in Spirituality, St. Louis, 1988).

"Spirituality of the Heart of Jesus," by F.J. Powers, S.J., 60-p. booklet (*Canadian Messenger of the Sacred Heart,* Toronto, 1990).

This book was designed and published by St. Pauls/ Alba House, the publishing arm of the Society of St. Paul, an international religious congregation of priests and brothers dedicated to serving the Church through the communications media. For information regarding this and associated ministries of the Pauline Family of Congregations, write to the Vocation Director, Society of St. Paul, 7050 Pinehurst, Dearborn, Michigan 48126. Phone (313) 582-3798 or check our internet site, www.albahouse.org